Lecture Lah...

Islam in Comp...
other Relig...

Ḥaḍrat Mirza Ghulam Ahmad
of Qadian[as]
The Promised Messiah and Mahdi
Founder of the Ahmadiyya Muslim Jamā'at

ISLAM INTERNATIONAL PUBLICATIONS LIMITED

لیکچر لاہور

Lecture Lahore
Islam in comparison with other Religions of India

© Islam International Publications Ltd

First Urdu Edition: Lahore, 1904
Reprinted in *Al-Ḥakam* Qadian, 1904
First English Edition: Review of Religions, Sept. &Oct., 1904
Present English Edition (New Translation): UK, 2008

Published by:
    Islam International Publications Ltd.
    'Islamabad' Sheephatch Lane,
    Tilford, Surrey GU10 2AQ
    United Kingdom

Printed in UK at:
    Raqeem Press
    'Islamabad'
    Tilford, Surrey GU10 2AQ

ISBN: 1 85 372 983 3

Introduction

About the Author

Born in 1835 in Qadian (India), Hadrat Mirza Ghulam Ahmad, the Promised Messiah and Mahdi[as], devoted himself to the study of the Holy Quran and to a life of prayer and devotion. Finding Islam the target of foul attacks from all directions and the fortunes of Muslims at a low ebb, he, as the Imam and the voice articulate of the age, undertook the task of vindicating Islam and presenting its teachings in their pristine purity. In his vast corpus of writings, lectures, discourses, religious debates etc., he argued that Islam was the only living faith, by following which, man could establish contact with his Creator and enter into communion with Him. He announced that God had appointed him the Messiah and Mahdi, according to the prophecies of the Bible, the Holy Quran and Ahadith. In 1889 he began to accept initiation into his Jamā'at, which is now established in over a hundred and eighty countries. He wrote more than eighty books in Urdu, Arabic and Persian.

After his demise in 1908, the Promised Messiah[as] was succeeded by Khulafā (Successors), who have continued his mission. Ḥaḍrat Mirza Masroor Ahmad, Khalīfatul Masīḥ V[at], is the present head of the Ahmadiyya Muslim Jamā'at and the fifth Successor of the Promised Messiah[as].

About the Book

Islam in comparison with other Religions of India, which is commonly known as *Lecture Lahore,* was written by the Promised Messiah[as] and was read out in his presence by Maulānā 'Abdul Karīm Sahib Siālkotī before a large gathering in Lahore on 3rd September, 1904. This lecture contains a comparative study of Islam, Hinduism and Christianity, and shows the teachings of Islam to be superior to those of other religions.

The Promised Messiah[as] says the reason for the deluge of sin in the present age is the lack of awareness about God, and this can be remedied neither by the Christian doctrine of Redemption nor by the teachings laid down in the Vedas. True and perfect awareness about God, which can only be attained through direct communion with the Almighty, can only be attained through Islam, for other religions have once and for all closed upon themselves the door to Divine revelation.

The first English translation of this lecture was published in the September & October, 1904, edition of *The Review of Religions*. This new translation has been prepared by Wakālat Taṣnīf, Rabwah.

Acknowledgements

I owe a debt of gratitude to the following for assisting me in the various stages of this translation: Raja Ata-ul-Mannan, Dhulqarnain, Syed Tanwir Mujtaba, Tahir Mahmood Mubashar and Professor Abdul Jalil Sadiq. I am also grateful to Munir-ud-Din Shams Sahib, Additional Wakīl-ut-Taṣnīf, for his help and support, and for providing the vital link for seeking guidance from Ḥaḍrat Mirza Masroor Ahmad, Khalīfatul Masīḥ V[at].

Chaudhry Muhammad 'Alī
Wakīlut Taṣnīf
Teḥrīk Jadīd
Rabwah
27th March, 2008

Publisher's Note

Please note that words in the text in normal brackets ( ) and in between the long dashes—are the words of the Promised Messiah[as]. If any explanatory words or phrases are added by the translator for the purpose of clarification, they are put in square brackets [ ].

The name of Muhammad[sa], the Holy Prophet of Islam, has been followed by the symbol [sa], which is an abbreviation for the salutation Ṣallallāhu 'Alaihi Wasallam (may peace and blessings of Allah be upon him). The names of other Prophets and Messengers are followed by the symbol [as], an abbreviation for 'Alaihissalām (on whom be peace). The actual salutations have not generally been set out in full, but they should nevertheless, be understood as being repeated in full in each case. The symbol [ra] is used with the name of the companions of the Holy Prophet[sa] and those of the Promised Messiah[as], and it stands for Raḍi Allāhu 'anhu/'anhā/'anhum (May Allah be pleased with him/with her/with them). Likewise, the symbol [rh] stands for Raḥimahullāhu Ta'ālā (may Allah have mercy on him), and [at] stands for Ayyadahullāhu Ta'ālā (May Allah, the Mighty help him).

In transliterating Arabic words we have followed the following system adopted by the Royal Asiatic Society.

ا at the beginning of a word, pronounced as *a, i, u* preceded by a very slight aspiration, like *h* in the English word 'honour'.
ث *th*, pronounced like th in the English word 'thing'.
ح *ḥ*, a guttural aspirate, stronger than h.
خ *kh*, pronounced like the Scotch ch in 'loch'.
ذ *dh*, pronounced like the English th in 'that'.
ص *ṣ*, strongly articulated s.
ض *ḍ*, similar to the English th in 'this'.
ط *ṭ*, strongly articulated palatal t.
ظ *ẓ*, strongly articulated z.
ع ', a strong guttural, the pronunciation of which must be learnt by the ear.

غ   *gh*, a sound approached very nearly in the r '*grasseye*' in French, and in the German r. It requires the muscles of the throat to be in the 'gargling' position whilst pronouncing it.

ق   *q*, a deep guttural k sound.

ئ   ', a sort of catch in the voice.

Short vowels are represented by:

a   for ─╱─ (like *u* in 'bud');
i   for ─╱─ (like *i* in 'bid');
u   for ─ؙ─ (like *oo* in 'wood');

Long vowels by:

ā   for ─ا─ or آ (like *a* in 'father');
ī   for ی ─╱─ or ─╱─ (like *ee* in 'deep');
ū   for ؤ ─ؙ─ (like *oo* in 'root');

Other:

ai   for ی ─╱─ (like *i* in 'site');
au   for ؤ ─╱─ (resembling *ou* in 'sound').

The consonants not included in the above list have the same phonetic value as in the principal languages of Europe.

We have not transliterated Arabic words which have become part of English language, e.g., Islam, Mahdi, Quran, Hijra, Ramadan, Hadith, ulema, umma, sunna, kafir, purdah etc.

For quotes straight commas (straight quotes) are used to differentiate them from the curved commas used in the system of transliteration, ' for ع, ' for ء. Commas as punctuation marks are used according to the normal usage. Similarly for apostrophe normal usage is followed.

THE PUBLISHERS

[Facsimile of the Title Page of the First Edition]

[Translation]
'It contains a cure for mankind'
Muhammad[sa] is the Guide and Lamp of both worlds,
Muhammad[sa] is the illuminator of time and space;
I cannot call him God, for fear of the Almighty, but I do swear:
He is the beacon who shows man the way to God.

Islam in comparison with other Religions of India
a lecture by
the Reformer and Imam of the age, and the Promised Messiah,
Mirza Ghulam Ahmad, Chief of Qadian,
which was read out before a grand Jalsa in Lahore,
on 3rd September, 1904.
Printed and published for Anjuman Furqānia, Lahore,
by Me'rājuddīn 'Umar, General Contractor and Secretary of the same,
and Ḥakīm Sheikh Nūr Muhammad, Munshī 'Ālam, proprietor of
Hamdam-e-Ṣehat. Printed at Rifā-e-'Āam Steam Press, Lahore,
for the benefit of the general public.

Today, while going through the 27th August, 1904, edition of *Paisa Akhbār*, I learned that a gentleman named Ḥakīm Mirza Mahmood Ahmad Irānī, who is a follower of someone claiming to be the Messiah, is presently in Lahore and desires to have a *Mubāhala* [prayer-duel] with me.

I am sorry to say that at present I am too busy to acquiesce to his request. Tomorrow, Saturday, is the Jalsa which will keep me busy all day, and the day after tomorrow I will be leaving for Gurdāspur to attend the court in connection with a law suit. I have been in Lahore for the last twelve days and nobody has approached me with such a proposal, and I cannot understand the meaning of this untimely request when I am about to leave and have not a moment to spare.

Let me, however, suggest to Ḥakīm Mirza Mahmood another clear method for arriving at a decision. I propose that the editor of *Paisa Akhbār* should publish the complete text of my article, which will be read in the Jalsa tomorrow, 3rd September, 1904, and that Ḥakīm Sahib too should write an article and have it published in the same newspaper. Let the people then read both articles and decide which of them is based on truth, honesty and cogent arguments, and which does not live up to these standards. This method will be free from the ills that result from most debates. And since I have not addressed Ḥakīm Sahib in my article, and have not even mentioned him, we will also be able to avoid the kind of resentment that such debates often give rise to. *Wassalām.*

                         Mirza Ghulam Ahmad of Qadian

بِسْمِ اللّٰهِ الرَّحْمٰنِ الرَّحِيْمِ

نَحْمَدُهٗ وَ نُصَلِّىْ عَلٰى رَسُوْلِهِ الْكَرِيْمِ[1]

Lecture Lahore

First of all, I express my gratitude to God Almighty for having made us the subjects of a benign Government, which does not hinder us from the propagation of our religious beliefs and removes every obstacle from our path by virtue of its principles of equity and justice.

Respected audience, today I am going to speak about the different religions found in this country, and I will try to be as deferential as possible since some people do not like to hear facts which go against their religious beliefs. It is obviously not in my power to remove their inherent prejudice, therefore, even as I speak the truth, I wish to be excused for any offence it might cause.

There are many religions in this country and religious rivalry is sweeping the land like a storm, but I have realized, through deep reflection and continuous revelations from God, that all this contention springs from the single fact that most people have lost their spiritual faculties and do not fear God. Heavenly light, which helps to distinguish truth from falsehood, has gone out from almost every heart, atheism is gaining ground day by day, and, while tongues utter the name of God and Parmeshwar, hearts are growing

---

[1] In the name of Allah, the Gracious, the Merciful. We praise Allah and invoke His blessings upon His noble Prophet[sa]. [Publishers]

3

more and more inclined towards agnosticism. All this is easily testified by people's practices which are far from what they should be. They do profess a great deal but never practice what they preach. Here I do not mean to question the sincerity of anyone who privately leads a life of piety, but, for the most part, people have failed to attain the object for which religion was made essential for mankind. Most people do not care for the purity of their hearts, true love for God, sympathy for mankind, and higher morals, such as meekness, kindness, justice and humility; and have no regard for purity, piety and righteousness, which is the soul of religion. Alas! even as religious rivalry grows, spirituality only continues to decline.

The purpose of religion is that people should recognize the True God Who created the world, love Him so much that every other love should grow cold in their hearts, be kind and compassionate towards His creatures, and strive to attain the utmost purity. This purpose is being neglected in this age and most people are practically following some form of atheism. They do not seem to be aware of the existence of God, and it is this lack of awareness that causes sin to be committed with more and more audacity. It is plain that unless we possess true knowledge about something, we cannot understand its worth and can neither love, nor fear it. All forms of love and fear and appreciation are born out of awareness, and the major cause of the profusion of sin in this age is man's lack of awareness about his Creator. The sign which distinguishes a true religion from others is that it opens up for the believers many paths to knowledge and awareness about God, which causes them not only to desist from sin, but, when they have seen the beauty and glory of the Divine, to fall in love with Him so completely that to them even a moment of separation seems worse than the torments of Hell.

Deliverance from sin and love for God is undoubtedly the highest object of man's existence, and forms the true happiness that is also called Bliss. Conversely, every desire that goes against the will of God, and every life spent in the pursuit of such desires, is like the fire of Hell.

The question now arises as to how man can find deliverance from such an infernal existence. God has told me that salvation from this abode of fire depends solely upon true and perfect awareness of Him. The lure of carnal passions, which is destroying faith like a flood, can only be countered by something equally powerful. So, in order to attain salvation, we need perfect knowledge and complete awareness of God, as only diamond can cut diamond. It doesn't require a lot of arguments to show that only true God-realization—*Ma'rifat*—can inspire love or fear. If a child is given a diamond worth millions, it will not cherish it any more than it cherishes a toy. And if a man is given honey which has been poisoned without his knowledge, he will eat it with relish and will not realize its danger. On the other hand, no one will ever consciously endanger his life by thrusting his hand into a snake pit or swallowing poison. Why is it, then, that people do not fear the death that must come upon them as a result of transgressing Divine commandments? I tell you that it is only because they are not as aware of the perils of sin as they are of the harmfulness of a snake or a poison.

No logic can disprove the fact that perfect knowledge prevents man from doing things that are likely to cause him injury or death, and in doing so he does not require any belief in any doctrine of Redemption. Even the most hardened criminal suppresses many of his desires for fear of being apprehended and punished. He does not break into a shop in broad daylight, while armed policemen are patrolling the area, even though he can easily lay his hands on thousands of rupees. Why? Is it because he has faith in the Redemption and is overawed by the doctrine of the Cross? No. He desists only because he recognizes the black uniforms of the policemen and is afraid of their shining swords, and realizes that if caught he will be thrown into jail. This principle applies even to animals. A charging lion never jumps into a fire even when it sees its prey on the other side, and a wolf never attacks a lamb whose watcher is standing by with a sword and a loaded gun. So, dear people, the true and tried philosophy is that man requires no doctrine of 'Redemption' in order to keep away from sin; all he requires is true knowledge and awareness. If the people of Noah had possessed true awareness, which inspires fear of God, they would not have drowned; and if the people of Lot had truly recognized their Lord, they would not have been showered with stones; and if the people of this country had been granted true awareness that makes hearts tremble, they would not have been ravaged by the plague.

Imperfect knowledge is also futile, because the love or fear that results from it is also imperfect. No one can derive any benefit from imperfect faith, imperfect love, imperfect fear and imperfect knowledge, nor, for that matter, can anyone be satiated by imperfect food. Is it possible to satisfy one's hunger with a grain, or quench one's thirst with a drop of water? How then is it possible for you—who lack resolve and put little effort in search of the truth—to receive great Divine blessings with the help of little knowledge, little love and little fear? Remember, God alone can cleanse you of yours sins, and fill your hearts with His love, and overawe you with His Majesty, and, such is the eternal law, that all this is granted only after man has attained perfect awareness—the source of all fear, love and appreciation. He who is granted perfect awareness is also granted perfect love and fear, and he who is granted these is granted salvation, for he is saved from all sins that result from audacity. In order to attain this kind of salvation, we do not need the blood of Christ, or Crucifixion, or Redemption; all we require is a sacrifice—the sacrifice of our own selves which our very nature demands. This sacrifice is otherwise known as 'Islam', which, literally, means to offer oneself to be sacrificed, or to willingly and completely submit oneself to God. The beautiful name 'Islam' is the soul of the Shariah and essence of all its commandments. It requires perfect love to readily offer oneself for sacrifice, and perfect love requires perfect awareness, and this is what the word 'Islam' signifies. God Almighty says in the Holy Quran:

$$\text{لَنْ يَّنَالَ اللّٰهَ لُحُوْمُهَا وَلَا دِمَآؤُهَا وَلٰكِنْ يَّنَالُهُ التَّقْوٰى مِنْكُمْ}^2$$

i.e., neither the flesh nor the blood of your sacrifices reaches Me; the only sacrifice that reaches Me is that you fear Me and adopt righteousness for My sake.

It should be borne in mind that all the teachings of Islam lead us to the single objective which is inherent in the word 'Islam', and, to this end, the Holy Quran endeavours to inculcate Divine love in our hearts. It reveals to us not only His beauty and glory, but also reminds us of His countless favours, for it is only through beauty and kindness that love finds its way into a person's heart.

The Holy Quran teaches us that, by virtue of all His excellences, God is One and has no partner. He suffers from no shortcoming. He comprehends all perfect attributes and manifests all holy powers. He is the Originator of all creation and Source of all grace. He is the Lord of reward and punishment, and everything returns to Him. He is near despite being far, and is distant despite His proximity. He is above everything, but we cannot say that there is anyone below Him. He is the most Hidden, but it cannot be said that anything is more manifest than He is. He is Self-Existent and everything subsists because of Him. He sustains everything but nothing sustains Him. Nothing has

---

[2] Al-Ḥajj, 22:38 [Publishers]

come into being or sustains itself without Him. He encompasses everything, but we do not know in what way. He is the Light of everything in heaven and earth. Every light shines through Him and every light is a reflection of His Being. He is the Lord of the universe, there is not a soul that is not sustained by Him, and not a soul that exists by itself. No soul possesses any power that has not granted by Him.

His favours are of two kinds. (1) Favours that are granted without any effort on the part of anyone. These have always been in existence, e.g., the heavens, the earth, the sun, the moon, the planets, water, fire, air, and all the particles of the universe that have been created for our sustenance. He provided for our sustenance even before we had come into existence, or had done anything to deserve them. Can one say that the sun or the earth was created on account of one's deeds? These favours came into existence before man was created and have not resulted from any of his actions. (2) Favours that are bestowed as a result of people's actions. These are too evident to require illustration.

The Holy Quran says that God is free from all defects and is not subject to failure or shortcoming, and it is His desire that man, too, should free himself of his weaknesses by following His commandments. He says:

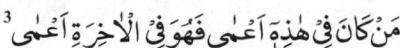

---

[3] Banī Isrā'īl, 17:73 **[Publishers]**

i.e., he who has no 'sight' in this world and is unable to behold the Peerless One, shall also be blind in the Hereafter, and darkness shall not leave him.

This will happen because the faculties that enable man to behold God are given to him in this world, and he who does not possess them and does not take them with him [to the Hereafter], will not be able to behold Him in that world either. In this verse God Almighty has clearly defined the progress He expects from man, and the heights he can attain by following His commandments.

In the Holy Quran, God has given us the perfect teaching, which, if truly followed, enables us to behold Him in this very life. He says:

$$\text{مَنْ كَانَ يَرْجُوا لِقَآءَ رَبِّهٖ فَلْيَعْمَلْ عَمَلًا صَالِحًا وَّلَا يُشْرِكْ بِعِبَادَةِ رَبِّهٖۤ اَحَدًا}[4]$$

i.e., whoever desires to see God—the True Creator—in this life, should act righteously. His actions should be free from mischief, ostentation, conceit and arrogance, and should neither be defective, nor deficient, nor contrary to one's personal love [for God]; and should instead be imbued with sincerity and faithfulness. He should also abstain from *Shirk* [associating partners with God] and should worship neither the sun, nor the moon, nor the stars, nor air, nor fire, nor water, nor anything else. He should also not put his faith in the physical means as though they were God's partners. Nor should he depend

---

[4] Al-Kahf, 18:111 **[Publishers]**

upon his own prowess, for this also amounts to idolatry—*Shirk*. Having done everything in his power, he should consider it of no consequence and should not pride himself on his knowledge or his efforts, and should think himself ignorant and worthless. His soul should always lie prostrate at the threshold of the Almighty, seeking His grace through prayer and supplication. Therefore, you should become like a thirsty and invalid person who finds a fountain of clear fresh water and tries to reach it stumbling and falling and, when he finally puts his lips to it, does not let go until he is fully satiated.

In the Holy Quran, God describes His attributes as follows:

$$\text{قُلْ هُوَ اللّٰهُ اَحَدٌ ۚ اَللّٰهُ الصَّمَدُ ۚ لَمْ يَلِدْ ۙ وَلَمْ يُوْلَدْ ۙ وَلَمْ يَكُنْ لَّهٗ كُفُوًا اَحَدٌ}$$ [5]

i.e., your God is One in His Being and in His attributes. No one is eternal and everlasting like Him, nor does anything possess attributes similar to His. Man depends upon a teacher for his knowledge, yet his knowledge remains incomplete, but God needs no teacher, for His knowledge knows no bounds. Man depends upon the air for his hearing which is limited, but God's hearing is inherent and unlimited. Man depends upon the light of the sun or other sources of light to see, and his sight is restricted, but God sees by His own light and His sight encompasses everything. In order to create, man is dependent upon matter and requires time, and his power of creation is confined,

---

[5] Al-Ikhlāṣ, 112:2-5 **[Publishers]**

but God's power of creation is not dependent upon matter or time, nor is it in any way limited. This is because all His attributes are unique like Himself, and if even one of them was flawed, they would all be considered flawed. His Unity—*Tauḥīd*—cannot be established unless He is seen to be peerless both in His Person and in His attributes.

In the final part of these verses, the Holy Quran says that God is not the son of anyone, nor does He have a son. He is Self-Sufficient and has no need of a father or a son. This is the Unity of God—*Tauḥīd*—which the Holy Quran teaches us and this is the basis of our faith.

Now we come to the ethical and moral teachings which the Holy Quran has laid out in this comprehensive verse:

اِنَّ اللّٰهَ یَاْمُرُ بِالْعَدْلِ وَالْاِحْسَانِ وَاِیْتَآئِ ذِی الْقُرْبٰی وَیَنْهٰی عَنِ الْفَحْشَآءِ وَالْمُنْکَرِ وَالْبَغْیِ [6]

i.e., God commands you to abide by justice and fairness. But if you wish to attain greater perfection, then treat people with compassion and do good even to those who have done you no good. And if you aspire to even higher perfection, then be of service to others out of personal sympathy and natural impulse, without any desire to win gratitude or to put anyone under obligation, and be kind to them just as a mother is kind to her children out of a natural urge. God also forbids you to commit excesses, to remind people of the good you have done them, or to be

---

[6] Al-Naḥl, 16:91 **[Publishers]**

Lecture Lahore

ungrateful to those who have been kind to you. This is further elaborated in the verse:

$$\text{وَيُطْعِمُونَ الطَّعَامَ عَلَىٰ حُبِّهِ مِسْكِينًا وَّيَتِيمًا وَّأَسِيرًا}$$
$$\text{إِنَّمَا نُطْعِمُكُمْ لِوَجْهِ اللهِ لَا نُرِيدُ مِنْكُمْ جَزَآءً وَّلَا شُكُورًا}^{7}$$

i.e., when the truly righteous feed the poor, the orphan and the captive, they do so selflessly, only out of love for God, and say to them: "We only serve you for the sake of God, from you we require neither gratitude nor reward."

With regard to retribution or forgiveness, the Holy Quran teaches us:

$$\text{جَزٰٓؤُا سَيِّئَةٍ سَيِّئَةٌ مِّثْلُهَا فَمَنْ عَفَا وَأَصْلَحَ فَأَجْرُهُ عَلَى اللهِ}^{8}$$

The retribution for an injury is an injury to the same extent. Tooth for a tooth, eye for an eye, and abuse for an abuse, but whosoever forgives—and the forgiveness results in reformation rather than mischief, and he who has been forgiven rectifies his behaviour and desists from evil—his forgiveness is better than retribution, and the forgiver shall have his reward [with God]. It does not teach us that, having been struck on one cheek, we should in all circumstances turn the other cheek also, for this goes against true wisdom. Doing good to an evil-doer can be as unjust as doing evil to a good man. The Holy Quran further says:

$$\text{اِدْفَعْ بِالَّتِيْ هِيَ أَحْسَنُ فَإِذَا الَّذِيْ بَيْنَكَ وَبَيْنَهُ عَدَاوَةٌ كَأَنَّهُ وَلِيٌّ حَمِيْمٌ}^{9}$$

i.e., if someone is kind to you, show him even greater

---

[7] Al-Dahr, 76:9-10 [Publishers]
[8] Al-Shūrā, 42:41 [Publishers]
[9] Ḥā-Mīm al-Sajdah, 41:35 [Publishers]

kindness. All rancour between you will thus turn into a friendship so close that it borders upon kinship.

وَلَا يَغْتَبْ بَعْضُكُمْ بَعْضًا ۚ أَيُحِبُّ أَحَدُكُمْ أَنْ يَّأْكُلَ لَحْمَ أَخِيْهِ مَيْتًا [10]

لَا يَسْخَرْ قَوْمٌ مِّنْ قَوْمٍ عَسٰى أَنْ يَّكُوْنُوْا خَيْرًا مِّنْهُمْ [11]

اِنَّ اَكْرَمَكُمْ عِنْدَ اللهِ اَتْقٰكُمْ [12]

وَلَا تَنَابَزُوْا بِالْأَلْقَابِ ۖ بِئْسَ الِاسْمُ الْفُسُوْقُ بَعْدَ الْإِيْمَانِ [13]

فَاجْتَنِبُوا الرِّجْسَ مِنَ الْأَوْثَانِ وَاجْتَنِبُوْا قَوْلَ الزُّوْرِ ○ [14]

وَقُوْلُوْا قَوْلًا سَدِيْدًا ○ [15]

وَاعْتَصِمُوْا بِحَبْلِ اللهِ جَمِيْعًا [16]

i.e., do not backbite one another: would any of you like to eat the flesh of a dead brother? Nor should a people ridicule another, proclaiming their own superiority and thinking of others as inferior, for those who are ridiculed may well be better than themselves. Surely, the more honoured in the sight of God is he who is greater in virtue and righteousness. The distinction of nation or caste is immaterial to Him. Do not call people with contemptuous names which they consider offensive, or else you will yourselves be considered evil in the sight of God. Keep away from idols and from falsehood, for they are both impurities.

---

[10] Al-Ḥujurāt, 49:13 [Publishers]
[11] Al-Ḥujurāt, 49:12 [Publishers]
[12] Al-Ḥujurāt, 49:14 [Publishers]
[13] Al-Ḥujurāt, 49:12 [Publishers]
[14] Al-Ḥajj, 22:31 [Publishers]
[15] Al-Aḥzāb, 33:71 [Publishers]
[16] Āl-e-'Imrān, 3:104 [Publishers]

Lecture Lahore

When you speak, speak wisely and reasonably and abstain from idle talk. Your whole body and all your faculties should be subservient to God, and all of you should together devote yourselves to His service. Allah also says:

$$\text{اَلْهٰىكُمُ التَّكَاثُرُ ۚ حَتّٰى زُرْتُمُ الْمَقَابِرَ ۚ كَلَّا سَوْفَ تَعْلَمُوْنَ ۚ ثُمَّ كَلَّا سَوْفَ تَعْلَمُوْنَ ۚ كَلَّا لَوْ تَعْلَمُوْنَ عِلْمَ الْيَقِيْنِ ۚ لَتَرَوُنَّ الْجَحِيْمَ ۚ ثُمَّ لَتَرَوُنَّهَا عَيْنَ الْيَقِيْنِ ۚ ثُمَّ لَتُسْئَلُنَّ يَوْمَئِذٍ عَنِ النَّعِيْمِ}$$[17]

O you who are unmindful of God, your desire for the world has made you heedless, and you do not relent until the time comes for you to enter the graves. You are wrong in doing so, and you will soon know. Indeed, you will soon know. If you possessed true awareness, you would see your own hell and realize that you are leading an infernal existence. And if you possessed even greater awareness, you would see with the eye of certainty that your life is indeed an infernal one. A time comes when you shall be thrown into hell and have to answer for all your indulgences and excesses and, having been overtaken by chastisement, shall reach the state of perfect certainty.

These verses show that there are three stages of certainty: The first is attained through knowledge and inference, as, for instance, when you see smoke rising from afar and infer through reason and deduction that there must be a fire in that direction. You reach the second stage of certainty when you see the fire with your own eyes. And you arrive at the third stage when you put your hand into the fire and

---

[17] Al-Takāthur, 102:2-9 **[Publishers]**

experience firsthand its property of burning. These, then, are the three stages of certainty: *'Ilmul Yaqīn* [certainty by knowledge], *'Ainul Yaqīn* [certainty by sight], and *Ḥaqqul Yaqīn* [perfect certainty].

These verses teach us that our true happiness lies in nearness to God and love for Him. The moment we turn away from Him and lean towards the world, we begin the life of hell, and everyone is bound to realize this sooner or later, even if he does so when he is at death's door and is about to leave behind all his worldly possessions and relations.

Elsewhere in the Holy Quran, God says:

$$\text{وَلِمَنْ خَافَ مَقَامَ رَبِّهِ جَنَّتَانِ} \;^{18}$$

i.e., anyone who gives up sin in deference to the honour and majesty of God, and in dread of the day when he shall be called to account before Him, for him there are two kinds of paradise. The first will be given to him in the form of a blissful existence in this world, where he will experience a holy transformation and God Himself will provide for him. The second paradise will be the eternal one, which will be granted to him after death because he feared God and preferred Him to all things mundane including his own egoistic desires.

$$\text{إِنَّآ أَعْتَدْنَا لِلْكَافِرِينَ سَلَاسِلَا۟ وَأَغْلَلًا وَسَعِيرًا ۚ إِنَّ الْأَبْرَارَ يَشْرَبُونَ مِنْ كَأْسٍ كَانَ مِزَاجُهَا كَافُورًا ۚ عَيْنًا يَشْرَبُ بِهَا عِبَادُ اللَّهِ يُفَجِّرُونَهَا تَفْجِيرًا} \;^{19}$$

---

[18] Al-Raḥmān, 55:47 [Publishers]
[19] Al-Dahr, 76:5-7 [Publishers]

وَيُسْقَوْنَ فِيهَا كَأْسًا كَانَ مِزَاجُهَا زَنْجَبِيلًا ○ عَيْنًا فِيهَا تُسَمَّىٰ سَلْسَبِيلًا ○ [20]

i.e., I have prepared for the disbelievers—who do not love Me and are inclined towards the world—chains and collars and a fire that burns in their hearts. Their feet are chained by their love for the world; their indifference to God serves as a collar for their necks, which does not allow them to look upwards but keeps them prone towards the world, and their hearts are constantly burning with craving for the world. As for the righteous, they are, in this very life, given a drink tempered with camphor—*kāfūr*—which cools their worldly loves and desires. They are given a spring from which this drink flows, and they cause it to flow into a running stream so that all who are thirsty may drink their fill of it. Once this spring has turned into a stream, and the power of faith has begun to grow, and Divine love has taken root in their hearts, the believers are then given another drink, this time tempered with ginger—*zanjabīl*. The camphorated drink they were given at first was only meant to cool the love of the world, and they now need a warming drink to set their hearts ablaze with Divine love. They need the second drink because the mere giving up of sin does not lead to perfection. The spring from which the drink flows is called *salsabīl,* which means 'Ask about the path that leads to God.'

قَدْ أَفْلَحَ مَنْ زَكَّاهَا ○ وَقَدْ خَابَ مَنْ دَسَّاهَا ○ [21]

---

[20] Al-Dahr, 76:18-19 [Publishers]
[21] Al-Shams, 91:10-11 [Publishers]

i.e., verily, he who purifies his self is released from the shackles of his carnal passions and is granted a heavenly life, but whosoever allows his self to get mired in the material world, and does not turn to heaven, shall languish in grief and sorrow.

Since it is not possible to attain these stages by our own efforts, the Holy Quran urges us again and again to pray as well as to strive. It says:

$$ اُدْعُوْنِیْۤ اَسْتَجِبْ لَکُمْ \; ^{22} $$

i.e., pray and I will accept your prayers.

$$ وَاِذَا سَاَلَکَ عِبَادِیْ عَنِّیْ فَاِنِّیْ قَرِیْبٌ ؕ اُجِیْبُ دَعْوَۃَ الدَّاعِ اِذَا دَعَانِ ۙ فَلْیَسْتَجِیْبُوْا لِیْ وَلْیُؤْمِنُوْا بِیْ لَعَلَّہُمْ یَرْشُدُوْنَ ^{23} $$

i.e., if My servants ask you what is there to prove My existence, and why they should believe in Me, tell them that I am very near. I answer anyone who calls Me, I hear his voice, and I speak to him. For their part, let My servants make themselves deserving of My converse and have perfect faith in Me, so that they may find My path.

$$ وَالَّذِیْنَ جَاہَدُوْا فِیْنَا لَنَہْدِیَنَّہُمْ سُبُلَنَا ؕ ^{24} $$

i.e., We surely show Our path to those who toil for it and make every effort in Our quest.

$$ وَکُوْنُوْا مَعَ الصّٰدِقِیْنَ ^{25} $$

---

[22] Al-Muʿmin, 40:61 [Publishers]
[23] Al-Baqarah, 2:187 [Publishers]
[24] Al-ʿAnkabūt, 29: 70 [Publishers]
[25] Al-Taubah, 9:119 [Publishers]

i.e., if you wish to see God, then pray and strive, and another requirement is that you should keep the company of the righteous.

These are the commandments that lead us to the true objective of Islam which, as I have said before, is that man should surrender himself completely to God, like a sacrificial lamb, giving up all his desires and intentions, and losing himself in God's will. He should bring about a virtual death upon himself, completely immerse himself in God's love, obey Him on the basis of love alone and for no other motive, and acquire eyes that see with Him, ears that hear with Him, a heart that is completely devoted to Him, and a tongue that only speaks when He speaks. This is the stage where the labours of a spiritual wayfarer culminate, and man's baser self is annihilated, and God's grace grants him a new life through His living word and shining light, and honours him with His sweet converse. The subtlest of lights, which neither reason can discover nor eye can penetrate, now draws closer to him by itself, as God Almighty says:

$$نَحْنُ اَقْرَبُ اِلَيْهِ مِنْ حَبْلِ الْوَرِيدِ$$ [26]

i.e., We are closer to him than his jugular vein.

It is thus that mortal man is honoured with His nearness and his eyes are given a fresh light that cures his blindness; he sees God with his new eyes, and hears His voice, and feels himself immersed in His light. This is the cul-

---

[26] Qāf, 50:17 [Publishers]

minating point of religion, where, having beheld God, man removes the soiled garb of his earthly existence and dons the magnificent robes of Divine light. It is not only on the basis of a promise that he waits for the Hereafter to behold God and to enter paradise, for in this very world he sees God, and speaks to Him, and partakes of the delights of paradise, as God says:

$$\text{اِنَّ الَّذِيْنَ قَالُوْا رَبُّنَا اللهُ ثُمَّ اسْتَقَامُوْا تَتَنَزَّلُ عَلَيْهِمُ الْمَلٰٓئِكَةُ اَلَّا تَخَافُوْا وَلَا تَحْزَنُوْا وَاَبْشِرُوْا بِالْجَنَّةِ الَّتِيْ كُنْتُمْ تُوْعَدُوْنَ}$$ [27]

Those who say that our God is He Who possesses all the perfect attributes and has no associate, either in His person or in His attributes, and remain steadfast, and their faith is not shaken by calamities or misfortunes or even when they come face to face with death, it is upon such people that angels descend, and God says to them, "Fear not these calamities, nor have any dread for your mighty foes, nor grieve over past misfortunes, for I am with you. Rejoice, for I will grant you in this world the paradise that you have been promised."

These statements are not without testimony, nor are these promises such as have not been fulfilled. There have been thousands of righteous Muslims who have tasted the fruits of the spiritual paradise in this life, and God has declared the true followers of Islam to be heirs to the diverse blessings that were given to all the righteous people of the past.

---

[27] Ḥā-Mīm al-Sajdah, 41:31 **[Publishers]**

Lecture Lahore

He has also accepted the following prayer which He has taught us in the Holy Quran:

$$\text{اِهْدِنَا الصِّرَاطَ الْمُسْتَقِيْمَ ○ صِرَاطَ الَّذِيْنَ اَنْعَمْتَ عَلَيْهِمْ ۙ غَيْرِ الْمَغْضُوْبِ عَلَيْهِمْ وَلَا الضَّآلِّيْنَ ○}^{28}$$

i.e., show us the path of the righteous ones, whom You favoured with every bounty, i.e., those who received every kind of blessing from You, who were honoured with Your converse, whose prayers were accepted, and who were accompanied by Your help and guidance; and save us from the path of those who incurred Your displeasure and forsook Your path.

This supplication, which we make in our Prayers five times a day, tells us that spiritual blindness does not only lead to hell in the Hereafter, but it also turns this life into hell. The truly obedient ones and the truly redeemed ones are those who recognize God and have perfect faith in Him, for they alone can forsake sin and immerse themselves in Divine love. A heart which has no desire to receive Divine communion is dead; a religion which cannot lead its followers to this perfection and fails to grant them communion with God, does not possess the spirit of truth and does not come from God; a prophet who does not lead his people on the path where they crave for Divine communion and God-realization, is not from Him and only attributes falsehood to Him; for the ultimate purpose of religion, which can rid man of sin, is to attain certainty

---

[28] Al-Fātiḥah, 1:6-7 [Publishers]

about God and the Day of Reckoning. But how can one attain this certainty unless one hears the voice of God—the most Hidden—saying 'I exist' and witnesses His manifest signs? Reason and logic can only go so far as to show, on the basis of the consummate and wise order of the universe, that the heavens and earth must have a Creator, but they do not go so far as to prove His actual existence, and the difference between 'should be' and 'is' is plain enough.

Amidst the current flood of religious rivalry, a seeker after truth must not forget that only that religion can be considered true which categorically proves the existence of God, and exalts man to the stage where he receives Divine communion, and saves him from the darkness of sin through its spiritual influence and life-giving quality. All else is mere deception.

Let us now examine some of the major religions of this country, and see whether they can lead us to certainty about God. Let us also see whether their scriptures contain any promise that they can lead man to Divine communion, and, if so, whether this promise has been fulfilled in favour of any of their followers in this age.

The religion which first requires our attention is Christianity. But it does not require a lot of analysis since the Christians themselves unanimously believe that all Divine revelation ended after the Messiah. For them revelation is only a thing of the past, all doors to it having been closed till the Day of Judgement. This is, perhaps, also the reason why they have devised a new way of achieving salvation, which falls short of all the norms of reason, justice and mercy. They claim that the Messiah agreed to take upon himself all the sins of the world and to die on the cross in order to bring salvation to others, and that God allowed His own son to be killed so as to redeem the sinners. But I fail to understand how people's hearts can be cleansed of sin by such an unmerited death and how the crucifixion of an innocent man can cause anyone's sins to be forgiven! This method is not only contrary to justice, but also to mercy; for it is unjust to punish an innocent person in place of the guilty one, and it is cruel to kill one's own son in such a callous manner, and that too in vain. The real cause of the current deluge of sin, as I have just mentioned, is lack of God-realization, and as long as the cause persists it is impossible to negate the effect. What kind of logic is it to say that although the cause—which is the lack of God-realization—is still present, the effect—sin—has been eradicated! There are thousands of instances in our experience which show that unless we have full awareness about something we can neither love it, nor fear it, nor understand its worth. Man's motivation for doing certain things and avoiding others is either love or fear, and these only come from awareness. Without awareness there will be no fear and no love.

Dear people, the truth compels me to say that the Christians do not possess anything that can lead a person to God-realization. They have already set a seal on revelation, their miracles have ended with the Messiah and his disciples, and they have abandoned the path of reason by deifying a human being. As for past miracles, which are now in the form of fables, their detractors might wonder just how authentic they are and how far they have been exaggerated, for the Gospel writers were used to overstating things. For instance, it is written in one of the Gospels that if all the works of the Messiah were written down, the whole world would not be large enough to contain them. What kind of logic is this! Is it conceivable that the world should be big enough to hold the actual works but too small to contain a written account of the same!

Moreover, the miracles of the Messiah[as] were no greater than those of Moses[as], and, if they are compared to the miracles of Elijah, the scale would definitely tilt in favour of the latter. If such miracles are reason enough for someone to be considered God, then these Prophets surely also deserve Godhood.

The argument that the Messiah called himself 'Son of God', or was described as such in the Gospels, also does not prove his Godhood. A number of people have been called sons of God in the Bible, and some have even been called 'God', and there is no reason why the Messiah should be singled out for Godhood. Even if Jesus alone had been given this title, it would be naïve to take it literally while Divine scriptures are full of such metaphors and there is no reason why the same distinction should not be conferred upon all those who share the title 'Sons of God' with the Messiah.

Again, the plan [devised by the Christians] for attaining salvation is not practicable, for it never stops people from sin, and it is a sin in itself to commit suicide for the deliverance of others. I swear by the Almighty that the Messiah never willingly accepted crucifixion, and the mischievous Jews had treated him as they liked. He spent the whole night weeping and praying in a garden, and God accepted his prayers on account of his righteousness, and—as the Bible itself admits—saved him from an accursed death on the cross. It is, therefore, sheer calumny to say that the Messiah willingly committed suicide, and it is unreasonable to suggest that one can cure the headache of another by striking one's own head.

It is our belief that the Messiah[as] was a Prophet and one of the Perfect Ones whom God purifies with His own Hand, but we can never ascribe Godhood to him, or to any other Prophet, on the basis of what is written about them in the holy scriptures. I myself am experienced in these matters. The praise and honour that God has conferred upon me in His holy revelations is far greater than what has been written about the Messiah. Would I then be justified in calling myself 'God' or 'Son of God'?

Let us now look at the teachings contained in the Gospels. I believe that a perfect teaching must nurture all of man's faculties, instead of emphasizing any particular aspect. I truthfully declare that the perfect teaching, which is always consistent with truth and wisdom, is only to be found in the Holy Quran. The Gospel teaches its followers: "Whosoever shall smite thee on thy right cheek, turn to him the other also," but the Holy Quran says that this teaching does not apply to every situation, and one must decide whether forgiveness or retribution is more suited to a particular situation. This is undoubtedly the perfect teaching which the world must follow if it is to save itself from confusion and disorder.

The Gospel forbids looking at women with lust, but the Holy Quran teaches us not to look at them unnecessarily, with or without lust, for this is likely to lead us astray. Should such a need arise, we should keep our eyes half-shut and avoid staring at them. This is the only way to preserve the purity of our hearts. Those who oppose us might also oppose this teaching because of their newly discovered freedom, but experience has already shown that there cannot be a teaching more appropriate. Listen, dear friends! No good can come out of the free mixing of the sexes and the exchange of lascivious glances, while we know that men and women are not free from their carnal passions. Indeed, it amounts to deliberately throwing them into a pit.

The Gospel also says, "No one should put away his wife, saving for the cause of fornication", but the Holy Quran allows divorce for a number of other reasons also. For instance, if man and wife become mutual enemies, and one fears the other for his or her life, or if the woman has been guilty of actions that lead to fornication without having actually committed it, or if she suffers from some fatal disease which the husband is in danger of contracting, and in other such cases, the Holy Quran does allow the husband to divorce his wife.

Coming back to the main subject, let me reiterate that Christianity does not offer any realistic means for attaining salvation or enabling man to abstain from sin. Salvation can only be meaningful if man reaches a state where he does not boldly venture upon sin, and his love for God becomes so strong that no egoistic passion can surmount it, and this, obviously, cannot be attained without complete God-realization. In the Holy Quran we find clearly defined ways and means for attaining knowledge about God, which generates fear and keeps one away from sin. Through obedience to the Holy Quran, man is granted Divine converse and heavenly signs and is given news of the unseen, and all this results in a strong bond between man and his Master. At this stage man begins to desire passionately for union with Him, and puts Him above everything else. His prayers are accepted and he is given the news of their acceptance beforehand, and a mighty river of Divine knowledge and awareness flows in his heart and stops him from sin. But when we read the Gospels, we find only one method [for attaining salvation], which, apart from being irrational, has nothing to do with the eradication of sin. It is indeed strange that even though the Messiah[as] exhibited all kinds of human weaknesses, and did not show any Divine powers which could set him apart from other mortals, the Christians still consider him to be God!

Let us now turn to the Ārya Samājists and see what they have to offer in the way of salvation from sin. Since the Vedas categorically reject the possibility of all future Divine converse and heavenly signs, it is futile to think that they can lead anyone to the point of certainty where he hears God's voice proclaiming 'I exist', or his prayers are answered, or God reveals His countenance to him through His signs. The Āryas consider all this to be impossible.

The fact, nevertheless, remains that love or fear is not possible without having 'seen' God and without having attained perfect God-realization—*Ma'rifat*. But the mere study of creation cannot bring about such certainty, and this is why many of those who profess to follow pure reason are atheists and agnostics, and those who reach the heights of philosophy are considered the true atheists. Reason, if it is not tainted with atheism, can only help us analyze the creation and conclude that it *must have* a Creator, but it cannot grant us any certainty as to whether there actually *is* a Creator. It may, on the contrary, lead us to believe that the whole universe is functioning on its own and that some objects have an inborn ability to create others, but it can never bring us the kind of perfect certainty or complete awareness which is equivalent to beholding the Almighty and generates perfect fear and perfect love.

The fire of love and fear consumes every sin, annihilates every selfish desire, removes all the stains of sinfulness, and cures every inner weakness through a pure and holy transformation. But since most people do not care for such

Lecture Lahore

perfect purity as removes all the stains of sin, they do not seek it and even oppose it due to their inherent prejudices.

We can only pity the Āryas, because they have not only lost all hope of attaining true God-realization, but do not even possess any rational argument to prove the existence of God. They surely cannot prove His existence while they believe every particle and every soul, with all its faculties, to be eternal and self-existent. It is also futile to try to prove Parmeshwar's existence by arguing that the particles need someone to assemble them and to infuse souls into them, for why should the particles require anyone else to do this when they themselves are powerful enough to have sustained themselves through eternity, and are virtually their own 'Gods'! Surely no one will accept that even though the particles or atoms do not depend upon anyone else for their existence and sustenance, nor are the souls dependent on anyone else for their existence and sustenance and their powers, they still require outside help to join or separate them! These beliefs do make the Āryas easy prey for atheists.

I also feel sorry for the Āryas because they have committed serious errors in both aspects of their doctrine. First, they believe that God—Parmeshwar—is not the source of all creation, nor the fountainhead of all blessings; and that all particles and souls and all the faculties are self-existent and have not partaken of His favours. In the context of this belief, can anyone tell us what is the use of such a Parmeshwar, why He should be considered worthy of worship, on what basis He should be taken as Omnipotent—*Surb Shaktīmān,* and how man can ever recognize Him.

How I wish my sympathy would touch their hearts, and they would go into seclusion to ponder over these matters. Almighty God! Have mercy on them, for they have lived alongside us for a long time; and draw their hearts to the truth, for all things are possible for You. Amin.

This is the first aspect of their doctrine in which they have done grave injustice to the Peerless Creator. Transmigration—the returning of the souls to this world in different forms—is the other aspect of their doctrine which relates to the creation. Despite all their claims to reason and rationality, the Āryas believe that Parmeshwar is a hardhearted being who punishes the souls for millions of years as a penalty for a single sin and keeps throwing them back into the cycle of transmigration even though they are not His creation and He has no right over them. Would it not be more appropriate to punish them for a specific number of years, as earthly governments do? Greater punishment can only be justified if one has equally greater right over the guilty, but when all particles and souls are self-existent and the Parmeshwar has no right over them—except, perhaps to cast them into repeated rebirths—He is surely not entitled to put them through such a long punishment.

In Islam, although God says that He is the Creator of every particle and every soul, and the Source of all their powers, their life and their existence, He still says:

Lecture Lahore 31

$$اِلَّا مَا شَآءَ رَبُّكَ ۚ اِنَّ رَبَّكَ فَعَّالٌ لِّمَا يُرِيْدُ۟[29]$$

i.e., they will dwell in hell for eternity, but this eternity should not be confused with God's eternity, it only means a long period of time after which His mercy will intervene, for He is the Almighty and does what He wills. This verse has been explained in a Hadith where our lord and master, the Holy Prophet[sa], says:

$$يَأْتِىْ عَلٰى جَهَنَّمَ زَمَانٌ لَيْسَ فِيْهَا اَحَدٌ وَ نَسِيْمُ الصَّبَا تُحَرِّكُ اَبْوَابَهَا$$

i.e., a time shall come upon hell when no one will be left in it, and its gates shall be moved to and fro by the morning breeze.

But the Āryas present God as a rancorous and unforgiving being whose fury is never appeased and who does not forgive sins even after putting the souls through the cycle of transmigration for billions of years. The same is true of the Christians, for, although they consider God to be the Creator of all things, they still believe that He punishes a single sin with an eternity in hell.

The question is, do the souls not deserve at least some mercy from Him Who created them? Is it not He Who placed in their natures the weaknesses that draw them towards sin, and is not He Who winds the clock of their existence to run as long as He—the Eternal Watchmaker—wills? Does He not share some responsibility for their sins? Likewise, is it just on the part of God to limit His own son's punishment to three days while He condemns other

---

[29] Hūd, 11:108 [Publishers]

souls to hellfire for eternity? Surely, this does not behove the Lord of Grace and Mercy. The punishment of the son should indeed have been greater, for, being the son of God and possessing Divine powers, He could have endured far greater punishment than weak mortals.

Hence, the same objection applies to both the Āryas and the Christians. Some Muslims also hold such beliefs, but these can never be attributed to the Holy Quran which categorically rejects them. Such Muslims are themselves answerable for these beliefs, just as they are answerable for the belief that Jesus[as] is alive and sitting in the second heaven, and they await his return even though the Holy Quran has clearly stated that he has long been dead and is among the souls that have passed away.

Further proof of the falsity of the concept of transmigration is that it is contrary to the true moral and ethical values. For instance, when a man takes a woman for his wife, how can he be sure that she is not his mother or sister or granddaughter who might have died earlier on? Would such a person not be breaking the Vedic law by contracting such a marriage? Such a situation could be avoided if every child was born with a written record of its parentage in its past lives, but since no such arrangement has apparently been made by Parmeshwar, would one not be justified in believing that He Himself desires to spread such evil?

We also find it difficult to understand what the transmigration of souls is really meant to achieve. Salvation—

muktī—undoubtedly depends upon God-realization—*gayān*—and if this is what transmigration is meant to achieve, then why is it that a soul loses all the stock of knowledge and awareness it has so laboriously earned in its past lives, and without which there can be no question of salvation. We see that every child comes into the world utterly devoid of knowledge, just like a spendthrift who has squandered away all his fortune and finds himself penniless. Even if one has read the Vedas a thousand times in his previous life, he will not remember even a page of it. It is hard to see how a soul can ever be delivered from the cycle of transmigration when it keeps losing all its stock of knowledge and awareness acquired in its past lives.

The souls are indeed ill-fated, for they do not only lack God-realization—*gayān*—to become deserving of salvation, but, according to the Ārya belief, their salvation also lasts a short period of time after which they are thrown back into the cycle of transmigration.

Neug is yet another aspect of the Ārya doctrine which is contrary to the purity of the human soul. I would never attribute this doctrine to the Vedas, and I believe that human conscience can never allow a man to make his chaste wife, who has her honour and comes of a respectable family, to sleep with another man merely in order to procure progeny. Nor do I think it proper for a woman to desire such a thing while her husband is yet alive. Let alone humans, even some animals have a sense of honour whereby they do not allow their females to mate with anyone else.

I do not wish to enter into any argument over this issue, but I do respectfully beseech the Āryas that it would be better for them to renounce this doctrine. Our country is already seriously lacking in morality and chastity, and if men and women were allowed such liberties, God only knows where things might end up.

Let me also venture to add that no matter how the Āryas hate the Muslims and detest the teachings of Islam, they should not altogether discard the custom of purdah, for this will result in many evils which will make themselves felt sooner or later. Every wise man realizes that the majority of people follow the dictates of their baser selves, and forget all about God's punishment when they are in the grip of their passions. Men do not desist from casting evil glances at beautiful women, and some women also do not hesitate to stare at men. If the two are given liberty to mix freely, while their hearts are not free from evil, the result will not be much different from what we see in some parts of Europe. People can only be allowed such freedom when they have become truly pure-hearted and have freed themselves of their baser selves, when the evil spirit has departed from their souls, the fear of God is apparent from their eyes, and His Majesty has been established in their hearts, and when they have undergone a holy transformation and donned themselves in the mantel of righteousness, for they will then be like pawns in the hand of God and will cease to be males, in a manner of speaking, and their eyes will become oblivious to the sight of women and no such thoughts will ever enter them.

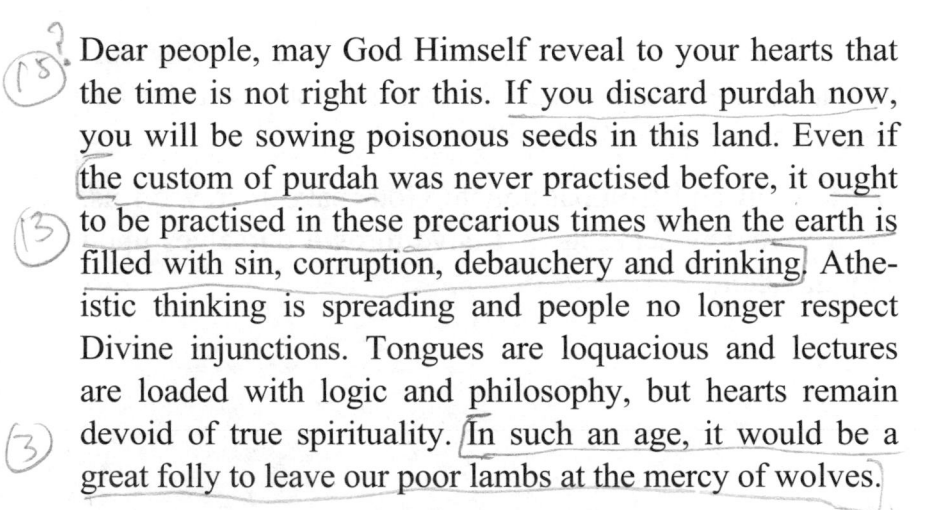

Dear people, may God Himself reveal to your hearts that the time is not right for this. If you discard purdah now, you will be sowing poisonous seeds in this land. Even if the custom of purdah was never practised before, it ought to be practised in these precarious times when the earth is filled with sin, corruption, debauchery and drinking. Atheistic thinking is spreading and people no longer respect Divine injunctions. Tongues are loquacious and lectures are loaded with logic and philosophy, but hearts remain devoid of true spirituality. In such an age, it would be a great folly to leave our poor lambs at the mercy of wolves.

Friends, the Plague is also upon us and, in view of the knowledge God has granted me, I believe that its ravages are far from over and there is still great danger. No one can tell who will be alive by next May and who will be dead, and which home will be devastated and which will be spared. Rise up, therefore, and repent, and appease your Lord with good deeds.

Bear in mind that the errors of belief will only be punished after death, and the dispute between Hindus, Christian and Muslims will be decided in the Hereafter, but he who crosses all bounds in audacity and immorality will be punished in this world, and there is no way he can escape Divine chastisement. Try to please your Lord before the great and terrible day comes, when the Plague foretold by the Prophets shall rage. Make you peace with Him and remember that He is the Most Compassionate and forgives the sins of a whole lifetime in a moment of self-consuming repentance. Do not despair of His forgiveness. Remember, that you can only be saved by His grace and not through any of your efforts.

O Merciful and Compassionate God, have mercy on us, for we are Thy servants and have thrown ourselves upon Thy threshold.

Part II

Worthy audience, I will now speak about my claim which has been communicated to the people of this country. Both reason and tradition testify that when the world is engulfed by the darkness of sin, the earth is filled with evil and vice, spirituality falls to its lowest ebb, the land becomes polluted with sin, love for the Almighty grows cold, and a poisonous wind blows over the land, at such times Divine mercy desires to resurrect the earth once again. This process is similar to the changing of seasons; in Autumn the trees are stripped of their fruit and leaves and flowers, and seem as unsightly as a man in the last stage of consumption with a bloodless visage, looking more dead than alive, or like a leper whose limbs have begun to wither; and then comes Spring when the same trees take on an entirely different hue and colour, and bring forth fruits and flowers and leaves that are so pleasing to behold. Mankind goes through similar phases of light and darkness. Some ages are like Autumn, in which human excellences lose all their shine and lustre, while others are like Spring, in which a heavenly breeze brings fresh life into people's hearts. These two phases have alternately influenced mankind since its creation.

The current age can be likened to the beginning of Spring. The deadness of Autumn was seen in the Punjab during the Sikh rule, when ignorance swept the land and religious books became so scarce that they could only be found in the libraries of a few noblemen. This was followed by the

British rule, in which we have enjoyed such peace and freedom that it would be wrong to compare even the days under the Sikhs to the nights under the British.

This age is attended by both spiritual and material blessings, and the beginning of this Spring holds great promise for the future. But, like a freak creature, this age also has many faces: some are ugly and frightful, for they are contrary to piety and God-realization; and others are blessed and auspicious, for they promote piety and righteousness. The British Government has undoubtedly advanced all kinds of knowledge and learning in this country and has introduced such easy methods for printing and publishing books that nothing like it has ever been seen in the past. Thousands of libraries that had hitherto been unknown have now come to light, and, in terms of knowledge and learning, the nation has been transformed beyond all recognition. But, notwithstanding all this, the practical condition of the people has deteriorated and the seeds of atheism have begun to sprout in their hearts. There is no doubt the British Government has done everything in its power to provide facilities to its people and to bring them justice and security, and it is hard to find anything like it under any other government, but most people have not been able to digest the freedom which is necessary for creating a completely peaceful environment, and, instead of being grateful to God and to the Government, have succumbed to indolence, worldliness, materialism and wantonness. They seem to think that they are going to live forever, and no one has done them any favour, and they

Lecture Lahore

do not consider themselves answerable to anyone. In keeping with the law that most sins are committed in times of peace and tranquillity, we find that sin has proliferated in this country and callousness and apathy has brought it to an alarming state. Rogues and mischief-makers—who are more beasts than men—are busy committing heinous crimes such as robbery, rape and murder, while others indulge in other kinds of vices according to their personal dispositions. The result is that taverns are faring better than other businesses, immoral professions are on the rise, places of worship are only used for rituals, the earth has been overwhelmed by a deluge of sin, and, just as whole villages are quickly inundated by a raging river that breaches its banks, so has peace and comfort caused people to be overwhelmed by their carnal passions. The earth has been enveloped by darkness and the time has now come when God will either bring light into the world or destroy it altogether. But the world still has a thousand years to survive, and all the new innovations that have been made for worldly comfort and well-being clearly show that God desires to bring about a spiritual reformation parallel to the physical revolution. The truth is that man's spiritual condition has deteriorated far more than his physical one, and mankind is in danger of coming under Divine wrath. Every sin is at its peak, spiritual powers are growing weaker and weaker, and the light of faith is fading out. Reason, therefore, demands that a light must come from heaven to overcome this darkness. Just as physical darkness is only dispelled by heavenly light, similarly, the light that illuminates the hearts also descends from heaven. Ever since God created man, He has ordained that, to unite mankind, He shall bestow the light of His awareness upon one of them at every time of need, and shall speak to him, and make him drink the cup of His love, and show him His chosen path, and grant him the eagerness to invite others towards the light, love and insight that has been given to him, so that they, too, may become part of him, and guard themselves against sin, and share his awareness, and attain the heights of piety and purity. In accordance with this time-honoured law, God has already foretold through His Prophets that, at the end of the sixth millennium after Adam—when a great darkness would envelope the earth, and the deluge of sin would inundate the land, and hearts would become devoid of love for God—He will breathe into a man the spirit of truth and love and awareness, just like in the case of Adam, without resorting to any physical means. And this man will also be called the Messiah because God shall Himself anoint his soul with His love. This Messiah, whom the scriptures also call the Promised Messiah, shall be made to stand up against Satan, and the final battle between the legions of Satan and the Messiah shall ensue. For this spiritual battle, Satan will come prepared with all his powers and all his progeny and all his resources. Never will the world have seen such a fierce clash between good and evil, for on that day the Satanic schemes and devices shall be at their deadliest, and all possible means for misleading mankind shall be at Satan's disposal. Then, after a great fight—which, you must remember, will be a spiritual one—God's Messiah shall emerge victorious, and Satanic forces shall be annihilated. Thereafter, for a thousand years, which have been described as the 'seventh day', God's majesty, glory, holiness and oneness shall prevail upon the earth. And this shall be followed by the end of the world.

Let it be known that I am that Messiah. Let him who will, accept me.

There are sects that do not believe in the existence of Satan, and they might wonder what I mean by all this. Be it known that man is drawn by two forces, the force of good and the force of evil. The Islamic Shariah attributes the first to Angels, and the second to Satan. This means that there are two forces acting upon man, and he at times leans towards good, and at times inclines towards evil.

I believe there are many in this gathering who view with disdain my claim of being the Promised Messiah and being blessed with Divine discourse, and look down upon me with contempt, but I can hardly blame them. Those who are sent by God always have to bear ridicule in the beginning, and it may be rightly said that a Prophet is not without honour but in the beginning of his mission. God's Holy Prophet and Messenger[sa], to whom the Holy Quran was revealed, who gave us the Shariah, whose followers we are proud to be, and upon whom the Law was perfected, was received in the same manner by his people. For thirteen years he led a solitary and helpless existence in Mecca, and suffered persecution and ridicule at the hands of his enemies, until he was forced to leave the city. Who would then have known that this helpless man was to become the Imam and leader of millions? Such indeed is the Divine law that, in the beginning of their missions, His Messengers are viewed with derision and only a few are able to recognize them. They must suffer at the hands of ignorant people and be slandered and mocked and abused until God opens people's hearts for their acceptance.

So much for my claim. The actual mission for which God has appointed me is to remove the estrangement that has come between man and his Creator and re-establish a relationship of love and sincerity between him and his Lord. He has also appointed me to put a stop to religious wars by proclaiming the truth, to create religious harmony, to reveal the religious truths that have long remained hidden from mortal eyes, and to display the true spirituality that lies submerged under the darkness of selfish passions. I have also been sent to demonstrate practically, and not just in words, how Divine powers enter man and how they are manifested through prayer and concentration. But, first and foremost, I have been sent to re-establish forever the lost belief in the Unity of God—*Tauḥīd*—which is pure and luminous and unadulterated by any form of idolatry—*Shirk*. All this will not come about by my power, but by the Mighty hand of the Lord of heaven and earth.

While God has taken upon Himself the task of my spiritual training and has inspired me, through His revelation,

Lecture Lahore

with a zeal to bring about this reformation, He has also prepared hearts that are ready to accept my words. Ever since God sent me, a great revolution has begun to take shape in the world. Even though the people of Europe and America are ardent believers in the divinity of Christ, their own scholars are now beginning to distance themselves from this doctrine. People who had for generations been infatuated with idols and other deities are now coming to realize the worthlessness of their gods, and, even though they remain unaware of true spirituality and still hold on to their rituals, they have managed to break free from many frivolous rites, superstitions and idolatrous practices and are virtually standing upon the threshold of accepting Divine unity. I sincerely hope that soon God's grace shall push them into the citadel of His true and perfect Oneness—*Tauhīd,* where one is granted perfect love, perfect fear and perfect awareness. This is not just wishful thinking on my part, for God Himself has informed me of this through His holy word.

God, in His wisdom, has brought about this change so that all the different people of this country may become one, and a morning of peace and harmony may dawn upon this land. The hope that all the religions will become one is in fact shared by all religions. The Christians believe that the time is near when all people will accept the divinity of Christ. The Jews, also known as the Israelites, are fervently hoping that these are the days for the coming of their own Messiah who will make them masters over the earth. Islamic prophecies also speak of the end of the fourteenth century as the time for the advent of the Messiah of the latter day, and most Muslims believe that the time of the dominance of Islam is at hand. I have also heard some Pundits of the Sanātan Dharam proclaim that the time is ripe for the coming of their last Avatar who will cause their faith to spread all over the world. The Āryas, even though they do not believe in prophecies, have also been affected by this wind of change, and are exerting all their efforts to spread their faith in Asia, Europe, America, Japan, etc. Oddly enough, even the Buddhists are beginning to cherish such ambitions. And, humorous as it may sound, even *Chūrās*, or menials, of this country have been stirred by the desire to protect themselves against the hostility of other communities and to at least protect their own faith.

A new wind is thus blowing in the land. Every religion and community is zealously striving for its own supremacy at the cost of others, and faiths are grappling with one another like waves in a tempest. This, therefore, is the time when God Almighty had destined to put an end to all religious differences and to bring all religions together into one fold. It is with reference to this time and age, when wave will fall upon wave, that the Holy Quran says:

وَنُفِخَ فِى الصُّوْرِ فَجَمَعْنٰهُمْ جَمْعًا[30]

In its context the verse means that when the world will become filled with religious wrangling, and religion will

---

[30] Al-Kahf, 18:100 [Publishers]

attack religion as a wave falls upon a wave, desiring to destroy one another, the Lord of heaven and earth shall bring about a new dispensation by His own hand, without resorting to worldly means, and shall draw into this dispensation all worthy and capable souls, who will then understand the true purpose of religion, and a new life and a spirit of true righteousness shall be breathed into them, and they shall be made to drink from the fountain of true God-realization—*Ma'rifat*. This world will not come to an end until this prophecy—announced by the Holy Quran thirteen hundred years ago—is fulfilled. Nor is this the only sign of the age when all people will be united under one religion, for the Holy Quran mentions many other signs, such as, the building of numerous canals flowing out of rivers, discovery of minerals from beneath the earth, profusion of worldly knowledge, availability of means for the mass publication of books (this refers to the printing press), invention of a new means of transport—which will render camels useless, make it easy for people to meet and communicate, and facilitate the spread of news and information—and the eclipse of the sun and the moon in the same month of Ramadan. The plague will also be a sign of that age, and it will be so severe that no town or village will be spared from its ravages and death will pervade the land making it virtually desolate. Some habitations will be completely wiped out, while others will be spared after suffering to an extent. These days will be marked by expressions of Divine wrath, because people will not accept the signs shown in favour of His

Emissary in that age and will reject His Messenger who will come for their reformation. In this age, we have seen the fulfilment of all these signs. Every sensible person will realize that God has sent me at a time when all the signs that were written in the Holy Quran have been fulfilled. Although I have only quoted the Holy Quran, these signs have also been mentioned in the Traditions. Another sign of the time of the Promised Messiah recorded in the Holy Quran is:

$$\text{اِنَّ یَوۡمًا عِنۡدَ رَبِّکَ کَاَلۡفِ سَنَۃٍ مِّمَّا تَعُدُّوۡنَ}^{31}$$

i.e., 'A day in the sight of God is like a thousand years according to your reckoning.' Since the days are seven, we infer from this verse that this world is also meant to last seven thousand years, counting from the particular Adam whose descendants we are. We learn from the Holy Quran that other worlds have existed before us, though we do not know what kind of people inhabited them. But it seems that an era of the world lasts for seven thousand years—as a symbol of which the days have been fixed at seven, each standing for a thousand years. We cannot say how many such cycles the world has gone through and how many Adams may have appeared in their own times, but it is certain that, since God is the Eternal Creator, the world must also be eternal as a species, though not in its forms and manifestations. Here, too, the Christians have erred, for they believe that God was eternally idle before He created heaven and earth some six thousand years ago.

---

[31] Al-Ḥajj, 22:48 **[Publishers]**

Surely no sensible person would accept this. But the Holy Quran tells us that God is the Eternal Creator Who, if He so wills, may destroy the heaven and earth billions of times and create them anew just as before. God has informed us that the present human race originated from Adam, our common ancestor who came after the previous 'races', and this human race has an age of seven thousand years, and that these seven thousand years are to God just as seven days are to man. It has been decreed by the Divine law that every 'race' has a life span of seven thousand years, and it is to highlight this fact that the seven days have been ordained for man. Thus, the time ordained for the children of Adam is seven thousand years, five of which had already passed by the time of our Holy Prophet[sa], as shown by the numerical value of the words of *Sūrah Al-'Aṣr*. By now six thousand years of this era have gone and a thousand years remain. It has been prophesized, not only by the Holy Quran but by many earlier scriptures, that the last Messenger who will appear in the likeness of Adam, and will be named the Messiah, will appear at the end of the sixth millennium, just as Adam was born towards the end of the sixth day. All these signs should suffice for a man of understanding.

According to the Holy Quran and other Divine scriptures, the seven millenniums have been further divided as follows: First millennium: for the spread of guidance and virtue. Second millennium: for dominance of Satan. Third millennium: for the spread of guidance and virtue. Fourth millennium: for the dominance of Satan. Fifth millennium: for the spread of virtue (this was the millennium in which our lord and master the Holy Prophet[sa] appeared for the reformation of mankind and Satan was put in shackles). Sixth millennium: for the release and dominance of Satan (this millennium extends from the end of the third century of the Islamic era to the beginning of the fourteenth). Seventh millennium: for the supremacy of God and His Messiah, spread of virtue and faith and righteousness, establishment of the Unity of God and Divine worship, and dominance of every virtue.

We are now at the head of the seventh millennium and there is no room for any other Messiah to come after this, because there are only seven millennia that have all been divided into good and evil. All Prophets have spoken of this division whether in passing or in detail. But the Holy Quran has mentioned it very clearly, and from this we deduce the prophecy about the Promised Messiah.

It is indeed remarkable that all Prophets, in one way or the other, have foretold about the time of the Messiah and the mischief of the Antichrist. In fact, no other prophecy has been made so frequently and with such consistency. But some people still doubt its authenticity and demand its proof from the Holy Quran. Had they given some thought to the matter and pondered over the Word of God, they would have found this prophecy so clearly mentioned in the Holy Quran that no wise man would ever doubt it. In *Sūrah Al-Taḥrīm*, for instance, the Holy Quran has named some individuals of this umma as 'Sons of Mary'. It first

Lecture Lahore

mentions their likeness to Mary and then speaks of the holy spirit being breathed into them, which means that after acquiring the status of Mary, these people will progress further and attain the status of the Son of Mary. It is in the same context that God Almighty initially called me Mary, as is recorded in *Brāhīn-e-Ahmadiyya*:

$$\text{يَا مَرْيَمُ اسْكُنْ أَنْتَ وَ زَوْجُكَ الْجَنَّةَ}$$

"O Mary, enter thou and thy friends into Paradise."

Later He said:

$$\text{يَا مَرْيَمُ نَفَخْتُ فِيْكَ مِنْ رُوْحِ الصِّدْقِ}$$

"O Mary, I breathed into thee the Spirit of Truth." (This meant that, metaphorically speaking, Mary was now pregnant with the truth).

And He finally said:

$$\text{يَا عِيْسَى اِنِّىْ مُتَوَفِّيْكَ وَ رَافِعُكَ اِلَىَّ}$$

"O 'Īsā, I will cause thee to die and exalt thee towards Me." Here I was exalted from the status of Mary and was named 'Īsā, or the Son of Mary, and the promise contained in *Sūrah Al-Tahrīm* was thus fulfilled.

It is also written in *Sūrah Al-Nūr*, that all the Khulafā' shall come from this umma, and it appears from the Holy Quran that Islam was to undergo two great trials. The first of these occurred after the demise of the Holy Prophet[sa] when Hadrat Abū Bakr[ra] became the Khalīfa, and the second was to be at the time of the Antichrist which would coincide with the coming of the Messiah. It is to seek refuge from the evil of this time that the Holy Quran has taught us to pray:

غَيْرِ الْمَغْضُوْبِ عَلَيْهِمْ وَلَا الضَّآلِّيْنَ ۝[32]

Another prophecy about this age is also found in *Sūrah Al-Nūr:*

وَلَيُبَدِّلَنَّهُمْ مِّنْ بَعْدِ خَوْفِهِمْ اَمْنًا[33]

In its context, the verse means that Islam, in the latter days, will experience a great turmoil and will be in danger of extinction, but God will re-establish it upon the earth and bestow peace and tranquillity after great fear. This is also borne out by another verse:

هُوَ الَّذِیْۤ اَرْسَلَ رَسُوْلَهٗ بِالْهُدٰى وَدِيْنِ الْحَقِّ لِيُظْهِرَهٗ عَلَى الدِّيْنِ كُلِّهٖ[34]

i.e., God is He Who sent His Messenger so that Islam may prevail over all other religions. This alludes to the time of the Promised Messiah, as does the verse:

اِنَّا نَحْنُ نَزَّلْنَا الذِّكْرَ وَاِنَّا لَهٗ لَحٰفِظُوْنَ ۝[35]

According to the Holy Quran, the time of the Promised Messiah[as] will be similar to the time of Ḥaḍrat Abū Bakr[ra]. The evidence I have produced from the Holy Quran

---

[32] "[Guide us in the right path; the path of those…] who have not incurred displeasure, and those who have not gone astray."
—Al-Fātiḥah, 1:7 [Publishers]
[33] Al-Nūr, 24:56 [Publishers]
[34] Al-Ṣaff, 61:10 [Publishers]
[35] "Verily, We Ourself have sent down this Exhortation, and most surely We will be its Guardian."—Al-Ḥijr, 15:10 [Publishers]

Lecture Lahore 51

should suffice for any reasonable person, but if someone considers it inconclusive, then he should also admit that the Torah does not contain any prophecy about Jesus[as] or our Holy Prophet[sa], for the words of those prophecies were not so precise and had caused the Jews to reject him. If the Torah had indeed contained a clear and unambiguous prophecy about the Holy Prophet[sa], which mentioned his appearance in Mecca, his name as Muhammad, his father's name as 'Abdullāh, his grandfather's name as 'Abdul Muttalib, his birth in the House of Ishmael, his migration to Medina, and the time of his appearance, there would be no question of any Jew rejecting him. In the case of Jesus, the Jews were faced with an even greater dilemma, and one would think that they were rather justified in refusing to accept him, for the prophecy contained in the Divine scripture had clearly laid down that the true Messiah must be preceded by the return of Elijah. Although the Messiah contended that the prophecy did not mean the return of Elijah in person, and only referred to the coming of someone in his likeness, the Jews took this to be an interpolation in the word of God and continued to await the return of Elijah. This example shows that the prophecies about Prophets are always somewhat veiled so as to make a distinction between the good and the evil.

Besides, claims that are based on the truth do not have only one kind of evidence in their favour, for they are like diamonds and shine in every facet. In the same way, my claim of being the Promised Messiah can be proved from whatever angle one may look at it.

Take, for instance, my claim that I have been sent by God and that I receive Divine revelations. These claims go back some twenty-seven years and were even recorded twenty-four years ago in *Brāhīn-e-Ahmadiyya*. Every reasonable person can see that something based on falsehood cannot persist for such a long time. However big a liar a man may be, he can never be so audacious as to keep up a lie for as long as it takes a person to be born until he becomes a father. It is equally inconceivable that God should help a man and cause his Jamā'at to flourish and frustrate the designs of his enemies, while He knows him to be a cursed liar who, virtually every morning for the last twenty-seven years, has been fabricating revelations and prophecies and falsely attributing them to Him. Another argument which vividly demonstrates the truth of my claim is derived from the prophecies revealed to me when I was all alone and no one even knew me. I was writing *Brāhīn-e-Ahmadiyya* at that time and none but God—the Knower of the Unseen—was aware of my circumstances. It was during a time of such isolation and anonymity, that God granted me some prophecies regarding myself, which I recorded in *Brāhīn-e-Ahmadiyya,* and they were published at that very time. The prophecies were as follows:

يَا اَحْمَدِىْ اَنْتَ مُرَادِىْ وَ مَعِىْ. سِرُّكَ سِرِّىْ. اَنْتَ مِنِّىْ بِمَنْزِلَةِ تَوْحِيْدِىْ وَ تَفْرِيْدِىْ. فَحَانَ اَنْ تُعَانَ وَ تُعْرَفَ بَيْنَ النَّاسِ. اَنْتَ مِنِّىْ بِمَنْزِلَةٍ لَّا يَعْلَمُهَا الْخَلْقُ. يَنْصُرُكَ اللّٰهُ فِىْ مَوَاطِنَ. اَنْتَ وَجِيْهٌ فِىْ حَضْرَتِىْ اِخْتَرْتُكَ لِنَفْسِىْ. وَ اِنِّىْ جَاعِلُكَ لِلنَّاسِ اِمَامًا. يَنْصُرُكَ

Lecture Lahore 53

رِجَالٌ نُّوْحِىْ اِلَيْهِمْ مِّنَ السَّمَآءِ۔ يَأْتِيْكَ مِنْ كُلِّ فَجٍّ عَمِيْقٍ۔ يَأْتُوْنَ مِنْ كُلِّ فَجٍّ عَمِيْقٍ۔ وَ لَا تُصَعِّرْ لِخَلْقِ اللّٰهِ وَلَا تَسْئَمْ مِّنَ النَّاسِ۔ وَ قُلْ رَّبِّ لَا تَذَرْنِىْ فَرْدًا وَّ اَنْتَ خَيْرُ الْوَارِثِيْنَ۔ اَصْحَابُ الصُّفَّةِ وَ مَا اَدْرَاكَ مَا اَصْحَابُ الصُّفَّةِ۔ تَرٰى اَعْيُنَهُمْ تَفِيْضُ مِنَ الدَّمْعِ رَبَّنَآ اِنَّنَا سَمِعْنَا مُنَادِياً يُّنَادِىْ لِلْاِيْمَانِ۔ اِنِّىْ جَاعِلُكَ فِى الْاَرْضِ خَلِيْفَةً۔ يَقُوْلُوْنَ اَنّٰى لَكَ هٰذَا۔ قُلِ اللّٰهُ عَجِيْبٌ۔ لَا يُسْئَلُ عَمَّا يَفْعَلُ وَ هُمْ يُسْئَلُوْنَ۔ وَ يَقُوْلُوْنَ اِنْ هٰذَآ اِلَّا اخْتِلَاقٌ۔ قُلِ اللّٰهُ ثُمَّ ذَرْهُمْ فِىْ خَوْضِهِمْ يَلْعَبُوْنَ۔ هُوَ الَّذِىْ اَرْسَلَ رَسُوْلَهٗ بِالْهُدٰى وَدِيْنِ الْحَقِّ لِيُظْهِرَهٗ عَلَى الدِّيْنِ كُلِّهٖ۔ يُرِيْدُوْنَ اَنْ يُّطْفِئُوْا نُوْرَ اللّٰهِ وَ اللّٰهُ مُتِمُّ نُوْرِهٖ وَلَوْ كَرِهَ الْكَافِرُوْنَ۔ يَعْصِمُكَ اللّٰهُ وَ لَوْ لَمْ يَعْصِمْكَ النَّاسُ۔ اِنَّكَ بِاَعْيُنِنَا سَمَّيْتُكَ الْمُتَوَكِّلَ۔ وَ مَا كَانَ اللّٰهُ لِيَتْرُكَكَ حَتّٰى يَمِيْزَ الْخَبِيْثَ مِنَ الطَّيِّبِ۔ شَأْتَانِ تُذْبَحَانِ وَ كُلُّ مَنْ عَلَيْهَا فَانٍ۔ وَ عَسٰۤى اَنْ تَكْرَهُوْا شَيْئًا وَّ هُوَ خَيْرٌ لَّكُمْ وَ عَسٰۤى اَنْ تُحِبُّوْا شَيْئًا وَّ هُوَ شَرٌّ لَّكُمْ وَ اللّٰهُ يَعْلَمُ وَ اَنْتُمْ لَا تَعْلَمُوْنَ۔

O My Ahmad, you are my purpose and are with Me. Your secret is My secret. You are to Me as My Unity and My Oneness. The time is near when people shall be made ready to help you and you will become known among men. The world is unaware of the status you have in My eyes. God will help you in every field. You have a place of honour with Me. I have chosen you for Myself. I will make many people follow you and you will be their Imam. I will inspire people's hearts to help you with their wealth, and financial support shall come to you from far off places.

People will flock to you from distant lands. You must not be impolite to them and must not grow weary of them due to their large numbers, and pray to God, "Do not leave me alone, You are the best Companion." God shall provide you with companions like 'the people of the bench', and do you know who they are? You will see tears flowing from their eyes and they will profess, "O God, we heard the voice of one who was calling people towards the faith." I shall make you vicegerent in the earth. People ask with disdain, "How can you have such a status?" Say to them, "My God possesses wonderful powers. He is not answerable to anyone for what He does. It is you who will be called to account for what you say." They say, "This is no more than a fabrication." Tell them, "All work has been initiated by God," and leave them to their frivolities. God is He Who sent His Messenger with guidance and true faith, so that it may prevail over all other faiths. They will contrive to blow out the light that God wishes to spread in the world, but He will bring it to perfection, i.e., He shall convey it to all the hearts that are ready to receive it, even though the disbelievers like it not. God will save you from their mischief even if people do not. You are before My eyes. I have named you 'Mutawakkil' [one who puts his trust in God]. He shall never leave you until He has made a distinction between good and evil. Two sheep shall be slaughtered, and everyone who is upon the earth must taste death. That which you consider to be bad may be good for you, and that which you think is good may be bad for you. Allah knows what is good, and you know not.

These revelations contain four grand prophecies: (1) The first is the good news conveyed to me twenty-seven years ago when I led solitary life. God told me that I would not remain alone and the time was near when people would come to me in throngs from far off places, and they would come in such numbers that I might grow weary of them or be unkind to them, and this, He told me, I must not do. (2) The second prophecy was that the people who would come to me would lend me much financial support. There are many people who can testify to these prophecies and to their fulfilment. I was all alone at the time when I recorded them in *Brāhīn-e-Ahmadiyya*, and I lived a solitary life in the little known village of Qadian. But, within ten years, people began to flock to me exactly as had been described in the Divine revelation, and started supporting me financially. To date, more than two hundred thousand have already pledged allegiance to me. (3) The third prophecy, which was implicit in the above two, was that people would try to destroy this movement and to extinguish this light, but all their schemes would come to naught. There is no cure for one who is bent upon disbelief, but the fact is that these three prophecies have been fulfilled as clear as day. To predict success and Divine support in favour of a person who has long lived in a state of anonymity and helplessness, and shows no sign of becoming the leader of millions or being offered thousands of rupees, is beyond the power of human reason and foresight. If someone does not believe this, let him produce a precedent. These prophecies become all the more unmatched when viewed in the context of the third prophecy, that people would try their utmost to stop their fulfilment, but God would make them come true. Anyone who looks at all these prophecies together, will have to admit that this is not the work of man, for man cannot foretell if he will even live to a certain age. (4) The fourth prophecy contained the above revelations related to the martyrdom of two of my followers. This prophecy was fulfilled when Sheikh 'Abdur Raḥmān was martyred on the orders of Amir 'Abdur Raḥmān, the ruler of Kabul; and Ṣāḥibzāda 'Abdul Laṭīf Khan Sahib was also martyred in Kabul at the behest of Amir Ḥabībullāh.

Apart from these, thousands of other prophecies have also been fulfilled. I once informed Maulawī Ḥakīm Nūruddīn Sahib that a son would be born to him with sores on his body, and it transpired exactly as I had foretold. I believe Maulawī Sahib is present in this Jalsa and anyone can ask him to swear on oath whether or not this is true.

Then, 'Abdur Raḥīm Khan, son of Sardār Muhammad 'Alī Khan, a chieftain of Malīr Kotla, fell seriously ill and his life was despaired of, but God informed me through revelation that the boy could recover through my intercession. So when I prayed for him out of heartfelt sympathy and compassion, the disease left him and he virtually returned from the dead. 'Abdullāh Khan, son of the same

Lecture Lahore 57

gentleman, was also struck down by a fatal disease and was close to death when I received glad tidings of his recovery, and he, too, recovered as a result of my prayers.

Signs of this kind are so numerous that if I were to relate them all this lecture would not end even in ten days. Nor are the people who have witnessed these signs few in number, for hundreds of thousands have witnessed them.

In my book *Nuzūl-ul-Masīh,* which is to be published shortly, I have enumerated a hundred and fifty signs of all sorts. Some of these appeared in the heavens and some on earth; some were related to my friends and others to my enemies, and have already been fulfilled; some of them concerned myself and some my children; and some were even manifested through my opponents without any involvement on my part. For instance, Maulawī Ghulam Dastagīr Sahib of Qasur challenged me to a *Mubāhala* [prayer-duel] in his book *Fath-e-Rahmān*, and prayed to God that whoever among the two of us was a liar may die first. No more than a few days had passed when Maulawī Sahib passed away, thus bearing testimony to my truth. There are thousands of others whom God informed of my truthfulness through dreams.

These signs are so clear and categorical that anyone who looks at them collectively will have no choice but to believe. And yet some of my opponents demand that I must cite evidence from the Holy Quran to prove my claim. Though I have already shown that the Holy Quran contains enough evidence to show that I am the Messiah, I believe that it is sheer impertinence to lay down such conditions. If it was indeed essential to produce specific prophecies from Divine scriptures, it would be impossible to prove the Prophethood of any Prophet.

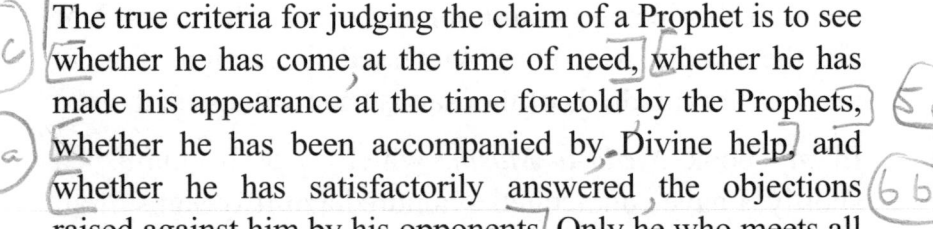

The true criteria for judging the claim of a Prophet is to see whether he has come at the time of need, whether he has made his appearance at the time foretold by the Prophets, whether he has been accompanied by Divine help, and whether he has satisfactorily answered the objections raised against him by his opponents. Only he who meets all these criteria can be considered truthful in his claim.

As far as the need of the time is concerned, this age is practically crying out for a heavenly reformer who will save Islam from inner dissension and external challenges, re-establish the long lost spirituality, strengthen the faith by granting certainty, save people from sin and transgression, and draw hearts towards piety and virtue. This shows that I have come at the time of need, and only the most prejudiced will deny this.

The second condition, that the claimant should appear at the time foretold by the Prophets, has also been fulfilled with my coming. The Prophets had prophesied that the Promised Messiah would appear at the end of the sixth millennium after Adam. The sixth millennium, if we go by the lunar calendar, has already passed; and if we go by the solar one, it is almost coming to its end. Moreover, there is the saying of the Holy Prophet[sa] that there would appear a Reformer—*Mujaddid*—at the turn of every century in order to revive the faith. We are in the 22nd year of the fourteenth century, and is it not a sign that the Reformer has come?

The third condition, that of Divine support, has also been fulfilled with my coming. People from every religion rose to destroy me, sparing no efforts and doing everything in their power to bring this about, but they were totally frustrated in their designs. There is no religion in this country which can take pride in the fact that its followers did not exert themselves to destroy me, but, despite all their endeavours, God honoured me and caused thousands to follow me. If this is not Divine succour, what is? Everyone knows how people of every community stood up against me, and how they all failed in their designs to destroy me, while I continued to grow by the day until I had with me a Jamā'at of over 200,000 people. Had I not been supported by a Hidden Hand, and had my mission been based on human contrivance, I would surely have fallen victim to one of the numerous arrows aimed at me, and would have been destroyed, and no one would even know where I was buried, because God Himself becomes the enemy of one who attributes falsehood to Him and there is no shortage of means for his destruction. But God saved me from all the designs of my enemies exactly as He had promised me twenty-four years ago.

It is undoubtedly a clear sign of Divine support that, at the time of *Brāhīn-e-Ahmadiyya*, when I was alone and lived in anonymity, God informed me in plain words that He would help me, give me a large following and frustrate the designs of my enemies. If you reflect with an unbiased mind, you will realize what a clear and outstanding sign this is. Does any man or devil have the power to make such a prophecy at a time of anonymity and to cause it to be fulfilled while thousands of people have risen up to stop it?

The fourth condition, that the claimant should satisfactorily answer all objections levelled against him, has also been fulfilled in my case. The major objection raised by my opponents was that Jesus[as] himself was to return to the world as the Promised Messiah. I told them that it is evident from the Holy Quran that Jesus[as] is dead and will never return to the world. For instance, Allah has quoted Jesus[as] as saying:

$$\text{فَلَمَّا تَوَفَّيْتَنِي كُنْتَ أَنْتَ الرَّقِيْبَ عَلَيْهِمْ}^{36}$$

When read in its context, the verse says that when Allah will ask Jesus[as] on the Day of Judgement whether it was he who taught his followers to worship him and his mother, he will say, "Lord, If I had done so, You would surely have known it, for You are the Knower of the Unseen. I only taught them what You commanded me, that God is one without partner and I am His Messenger. I was only aware of their condition as long as I lived among them, but ever since You caused me to die, You have been witness over them, and I know not what they did after me."

---

[36] "But since Thou didst cause me to die, Thou hast been the Watcher over them."—Al-Mā'idah, 5:118 [Publishers]

It is evident from these verses that Jesus[as] will say, "As long as I lived, the Christians did not go astray, but when I died, I knew not what became of them." Hence, if we suppose that Jesus[as] is still alive, then we will also have to believe that the Christians have not yet gone astray and are still following the true religion. Jesus[as] will also defend himself by saying that he only knew about the condition of his people as long as he was with them, but was unaware of what they did after God had caused him to die. So, if we believe that Jesus will return to the world once again before the day of resurrection and fight the infidels alongside the Mahdi, then—God forbid—we will have to consider this verse as false, or else we will have to admit that Jesus[as] will lie to God on the Day of Judgement and try to conceal the fact that he had returned to the world and fought the Christians for forty years together with the Mahdi. Anyone who truly believes in the Holy Quran will find that this single verse is enough to negate the concept of Jesus returning from heaven in order to fight alongside a bloodthirsty Mahdi. Whoever holds such a belief forsakes the Holy Quran.

When the objections of my opponents are thus countered, they, as a last resort, start alleging that my prophecies have not been fulfilled, and to prove their point they cite my prophecy about Ātham. Where is Ātham? The essence of my prophecy was that the liar would die in the lifetime of the true one, so Ātham is dead and I am still alive. The fact is that the fulfilment of this prophecy was conditional, and as long as Ātham lived in awe of this prophecy he lived up to the condition and was, therefore, granted a few months of respite. Those who raise such objections do not seem to remember that the prophecy made by Prophet Jonah was also not fulfilled, even though it is evident from the Book of Jonah that the prophecy was not conditional. The fact is that prophecies about impending punishment are not categorical and are conditional upon repentance, charity, alms-giving, prayer and even fear—all of which can either delay the punishment or avert it altogether. If this was not so, we could not consider Jonah to be a Prophet of God as his prophecy had not be fulfilled. When God intends to punish a transgressor, the punishment can be averted through charity and alms-giving, and even through fear. So, a 'warning prophecy' only means that God has decided to punish a person and has disclosed His intention to His Prophet, it is, therefore, foolish to think that a prophecy can be averted through alms-giving, charity and prayer when it has not been disclosed to a Prophet, but not when it has been so disclosed. Such an assertion amounts to an attack on all Prophets.

Moreover, some prophecies are not very explicit and their meaning only becomes clear with time. Even a Prophet might at times err in the interpretation of a prophecy, and this is nothing to object to, for Prophets are only human. Jesus[as] once said that his twelve disciples would sit on twelve thrones in paradise, but this did not come to pass, for one of them became an apostate and was destined for hell. Jesus also said that some people of his time would yet be alive when he returned, but this also did not happen. Many other prophecies made by Jesus[as] similarly remained unfulfilled due to errors of interpretation.

On the other hand, if someone listens to my prophecies with patience and sincerity, he will find that more than a hundred thousand signs and prophecies have been manifested in my favour. It is sheer insolence to ignore thousands of prophecies that have been fulfilled and to raise an uproar about one that has not been understood and to settle the issue on the strength of this alone. I hope, indeed I am sure, that anyone who comes to stay with me for forty days will himself witness a sign. I now conclude this lecture with the hope that what I have said will suffice for a seeker after truth.

وَ السَّلَامُ عَلٰى مَنِ اتَّبَعَ الْهُدٰى [37]

MIRZA GHULAM AHMAD OF QADIAN

---

[37] Peace be on him who follows the guidance. [Publishers]

Note

One, Ḥakīm Mirza Mahmood Irānī, in his letter dated 2nd September, 1902, has asked me to explain the meaning of the verse:

$$وَجَدَهَا تَغْرُبُ فِىْ عَيْنٍ حَمِئَةٍ$$ [38]

First of all, let it be clear that this verse holds so many secrets that it is impossible to encompass them all, and under the apparent meaning of this verse lie meanings that are not so easily understood. The meaning which God has disclosed to me is that when this verse is read along with the preceding and following verses, it constitutes a prophecy about the Promised Messiah and specifies the time of his advent. To elaborate this point, let me say that the Promised Messiah is also Dhulqarnain, because the Arabic word *qarn* connotes a century, and this verse indicates that the birth and advent of the Promised Messiah will span two centuries. And this clearly applies to me, for I have lived in two centuries according to every calendar I know of, be it Islamic, Christian or Bikrami, and my birth and advent have not been confined to a single century, and, in this sense, I am Dhulqarnain. In some Traditions, too, the Promised Messiah has been called Dhulqarnain in this very sense.

---

[38] "He found it setting in a pool of murky water."
—Al-Kahf, 18:87 [Publishers]

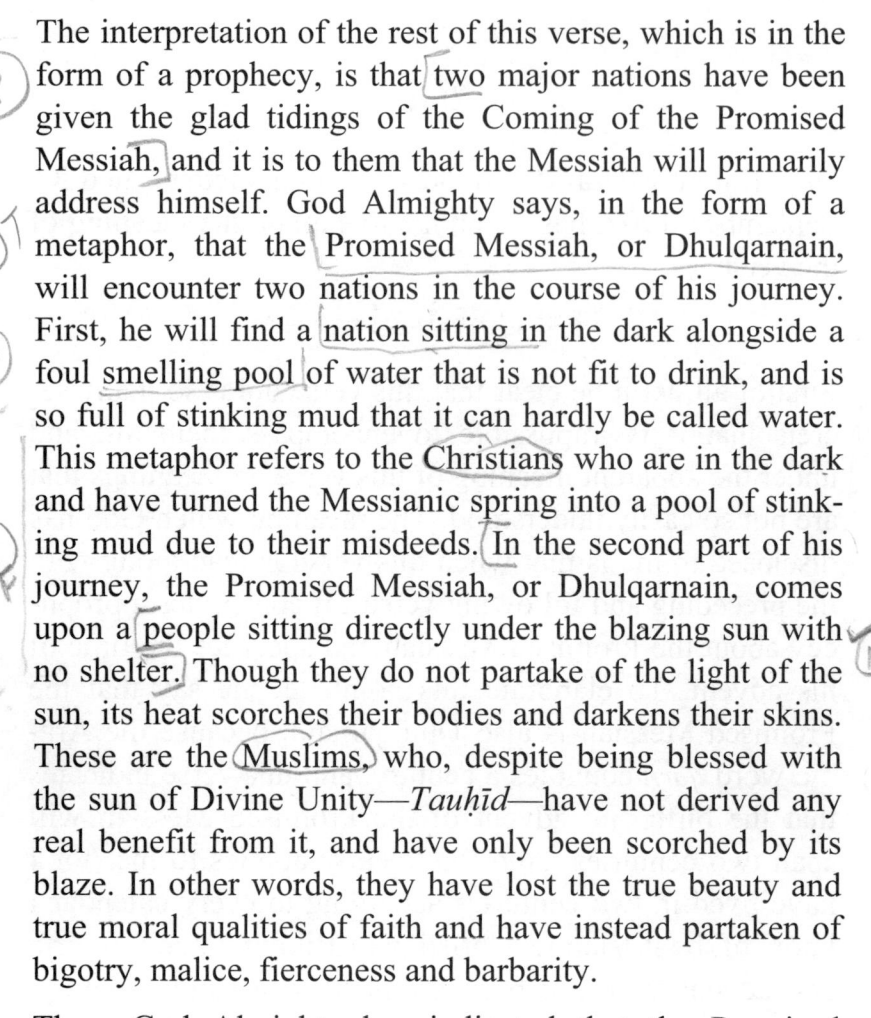

The interpretation of the rest of this verse, which is in the form of a prophecy, is that two major nations have been given the glad tidings of the Coming of the Promised Messiah, and it is to them that the Messiah will primarily address himself. God Almighty says, in the form of a metaphor, that the Promised Messiah, or Dhulqarnain, will encounter two nations in the course of his journey. First, he will find a nation sitting in the dark alongside a foul smelling pool of water that is not fit to drink, and is so full of stinking mud that it can hardly be called water. This metaphor refers to the Christians who are in the dark and have turned the Messianic spring into a pool of stinking mud due to their misdeeds. In the second part of his journey, the Promised Messiah, or Dhulqarnain, comes upon a people sitting directly under the blazing sun with no shelter. Though they do not partake of the light of the sun, its heat scorches their bodies and darkens their skins. These are the Muslims, who, despite being blessed with the sun of Divine Unity—*Tauḥīd*—have not derived any real benefit from it, and have only been scorched by its blaze. In other words, they have lost the true beauty and true moral qualities of faith and have instead partaken of bigotry, malice, fierceness and barbarity.

Thus, God Almighty has indicated that the Promised Messiah, who is Dhulqarnain, will appear at a time when the Christians will be in darkness, and stinking mud—which is *ḥama'* in Arabic—will be their lot, and the Muslims will have only a superficial belief in the Unity of

God, and will suffer from the sunburns of bigotry and barbarity, with no spiritual values left intact.

Then, the Messiah, who is Dhulqarnain, will come across a third people who will be suffering at the hands of Gog and Magog. These people will be deeply religious and pious by nature, and will seek the help of Dhulqarnain (the Promised Messiah) against the aggression of Gog and Magog. He will erect a bright rampart for them, i.e., he will teach them strong arguments in support of Islam which will finally repulse the attacks of Gog and Magog. He will wipe their tears, help them in every way and will stand by them. These are the people who accept me.

This is a grand prophecy which tells about my advent, my time and my Jamā'at. Blessed is he who reads these prophecies with care. The Holy Qur'an contains many prophecies of this kind whereby it speaks about someone in the past, but its purpose is to give news about the future. *Sūrah Yūsuf*, for instance, is only a narrative on the face of it, but it contains the hidden prophecy that just as Joseph was initially looked down upon by his brothers but was made their chief in the end, the same will happen to the Quraish. They rejected the Holy Prophet[sa] and expelled him from Mecca, but he who had been rejected became their leader and their chief.

Although the Holy Quran contains repeated prophecies about the Promised Messiah, i.e., myself, people who lack spiritual insight still say that the Holy Book does not mention the Promised Messiah at all. Such people are much like the Christians who to this day insist that the Bible contains no prophecy about the Holy Prophet[sa].

چشم بازو گوش بازو ایں ذکا خیرہ ام از چشم بند ئی خدا
ایں گماں از تیر ہاپُر ساختہ صید نزدیک است دور انداختہ [39]

MIRZA GHULAM AHMAD OF QADIAN

---

[39] *Their eyes and ears are open and their minds are sharp,*
But I am amazed that they do not see God;
Their bow has a large supply of arrows,
And the quarry is near, but they are aiming too far. **[Publishers]**

Index of Quranic Verses

1:6-7 19	33:71 12
2:187 16	40:61 16
3:104 12	41:31 18
5:118 58	41:35 12
9:119 17	42:41 11
11:108 29	49:12 12
15:10 48	49:13 12
16:91 10	49:14 12
17:73 8	50:17 18
18:87 63	55:47 14
18:100 42	61:10 48
18:111 8	76:5-7 15
22:31 12	76:9-10 11
22:38 6	76:18-19 15
22:48 44	91:10-11 16
24:56 48	102:2-9 13
29:70 17	112:2-5 9

Name and Subject Index

A

'Abdul Laṭīf Khan, Ṣāḥibzāda: martyrdom of, 62
'Abdul Muṭṭalib, Ḥaḍrat, 57
'Abdullāh Khan: miraculous recovery of, 63
'Abdullāh, Ḥaḍrat, 57
'Abdur Raḥīm Khan: miraculous recovery from a fatal illness, 63
'Abdur Raḥmān, Amir of Kabul, 62
'Abdur Raḥmān, Sheikh: martyrdom of, 62
Abū Bakr[ra], Ḥaḍrat, 55; the time of the Promised Messiah is similar to that of, 56
Adam[as], 44, 51, 65; may have been preceded by many other Adams, 51; the Promised Messiah was to come in the likeness of, 52
Afghanistan, martyrs of, 62
Allah. *See* God Almighty
America, 47, 48
Angels: Islamic concept of, 45
Antichrist, the: prophecies about, 53, 55
Ārya Samājists, 36; concept of salvation, 30; doctrine of *Neug*, 36
Asia, 48
Ātham: the Promised Messiah's[as] prophecy regarding, 69

B

Brāhīn-e-Aḥmadiyya, 54, 58, 61, 67
British Government in India, 3, 42
Buddhists, 48

C

Certainty: by knowledge (*'Ilmul Yaqīn*), 16; by sight (*'Ainul Yaqīn*), 17; perfect, (*Ḥaqqul Yaqīn*), 17
Charity: impending punishment can be averted through, 69
Christianity, 24; concept of salvation in, 24, 29

D

Dhulqarnain, 73, 75; the Promised Messiah is, 74

Divine favours: are of two kinds, 9
Divorce: Christian and Islamic teachings regarding, 28
Dreams: thousands were told of the truth of the Promised Messiah[as] through, 64

E

Eclipse, solar and lunar: a sign of the time of the Promised Messiah, 50
Elijah: miracles shown by , were greater than those of the Messiah, 26; was supposed to return before the Messiah, 57
Europe, 37, 47, 48

F

Fath-e-Rahmān, 64
Forgiveness: Christian and Islamic teachings regarding, 14, 27

G

Ghulam Dastagīr Sahib of Qasur, Maulawī: invitation to Mubāhala by, 64
God Almighty: attributes of, 9, 12; distinction of nation or caste is immaterial to, 15; is free from all shortcomings, 10; only , can cleanse man of his sins, 7; *Tauhīd* or Unity of, 12; to love , is the highest object of man's existence, 5
God-realization, 5, 23, 24, 25, 29, 30, 31, 35, 36, 42, 49
Gog and Magog, 75
Gospel writers: exaggeration by, 25
Gurdāspur, 9

H

Habībullāh, Amir of Kabul, 63
Hell: souls will not abide in , forever, 33

I

Ishmael, House of, 57
Islam: concept of Angels and Satan in, 45; destined to undergo two great trials, 55; does not say that souls will dwell in hell forever, 33; meaning of, 8; purpose of, 20; teaching about forgiveness and retribution in, 14; true followers of , are heirs to all the blessings given to past peoples, 22

J

Japan, 48

Jesus[as]: common Muslim belief that, is sitting in heaven in his physical body, 34; is dead and will never return to the world, 67; not the only one called 'Son of God' and the title does not make him deserving of Godhood, 26; prophecy about, in the Torah, 56; rejected by the Jews since the prophecy about Elijah was not fulfilled literally, 57; some of his prophecies remained unfulfilled, 70

Jews, 26, 57; eagerly awaiting the coming of their Messiah, 48; justification for rejecting the Messiah, 57

Jonah[as]: prophecy made by, remained unfulfilled, 69

K

kāfūr (camphor), 18

L

Lahore, 9

M

Ma'rifat. See God-realization

Mahdi, the Promised, 68

Mahmood Ahmad Irānī, Mirza, 9, 73

Malīr Kotla, 63

Martyrs of Afghanistan, 62

Mary[as], 54

Mecca, 46, 57, 76

Medina, 57

Messiah, the Promised, 44, 56, 58; is also Dhulqarnain, 74; Jesus[as] was to return to the world in the person of, 67; prophecies about the coming of, 53, 73, 76; signs relating to the coming of, 51; was to appear at the end of the sixth millennium, 65

Miracles: of the Messiah were no greater than those of Moses or Elijah, 25

Moses[as], 25

Mubāhala, 9, 64

Muhammad 'Alī Khan, Sardār, 63

Muhammad[sa], the Holy Prophet, 33; appeared in the fifth millennium after Adam, 52; foretold about the coming of a Reformer at the head of each

century, 66; persecution suffered by, 46, 76; prophecy about , in the Torah, 56
Mujaddid, 66
Muslims, 21, 34, 37, 38, 74, 75; most , believe that Islam will soon prevail over the world, 48

N

Neug: Ārya doctinre of, 36
Noah[as], 7
Nūruddīn Sahib, Maulawī Ḥakīm, 63
Nuzūl-ul-Masīḥ, 64

P

Paisa Akhbār, 9
Paradise: true believers are granted , both in this world and in the Hereafter, 17, 21
Plague, the, 7; a sign of the time of the Promised Messiah, 50
Prayer, 9, 11, 22, 47, 69; can avert impending punishment, 70
Prayer duel. *See* Mubāhala
Prophecies: about Ātham, 69; about impending punishment can be averted through prayer, alms-giving and repentance, 69; about Jesus[as] and the Holy Prophet[sa] in the Torah, 56; about the Antichrist, 53; about the latter days, 55; about the Promised Messiah, 48, 53; made by the Promised Messiah[as] and their fulfilment, 58, 61; specific , are not essential to prove the claim of a Prophet, 64
Prophet: criteria for judging the claim of a, 65
Purdah: importance of, 37

Q

Qadian, 61
Quraish, 76
Quran, the Holy, 8, 9, 10, 11, 13, 14, 17, 19, 22, 27, 28, 29, 34, 46, 49, 50, 51, 52, 53, 54, 55, 56, 64, 67, 68, 76; contains the perfect teaching through which one can see God, 10; moral and ethical teachings of, 13; speaks of the existence of other worlds before us, 51; teaching about Divine Unity, 12; teaching about forgiveness and retribution, 14

Name and Subject Index

R

Reincarnation, doctrine of, 32, 33, 35
Religion: distinction of a true, 5, 23; growing rivalry between religions, 3; purpose of, 4, 21, 22

S

salsabīl, 18
Salvation: Ārya Samājists' concept of, 35; Christian concept of, 24, 26, 29; how to attain, 5, 7, 8, 29
Sanātan Dharam: also expecting the appearance of the last Avatar, 48
Satan, 44, 53; Islamic concept of, 45
Sikh rule in the Punjab, 42
Son of God: a title given to many people, 26; being called , is no reason to ascribe Godhood to anyone, 26
Sūrah Al-'Aṣr, 52
Sūrah Al-Nūr, 55
Sūrah Al-Taḥrīm, 54, 55
Sūrah Yūsuf, 75

T

Tauḥīd (Divine Unity), 12, 47, 74
Torah, the, 56, 57

V

Vedas, the, 35; doctrine of *Neug* can never be attributed to, 36; rejects the possibility of all future Revelation, 30

Z

zanjabīl (ginger), 18